# Math Practice
# Grades 7-8

## A Best Value Book™

Written by
Kelley Wingate Levy

Edited by
Aaron Levy

© Carson-Dellosa CD-3750

ISBN 0-88724-531-5

# Table of Contents

# Resource Pages

The drill pages in this book are designed to evaluate a student's ability based solely on current knowledge of the material. Most drill pages, therefore, do not include explanations or examples of exercises. The following resource pages contain supplementary information relevant to the types of problems students will encounter in this book. Representative problems are broken into steps and solved, and are accompanied by descriptions of the processes involved. Students, teachers, and parents are encouraged to refer to these resource pages for instruction and clarification of concepts presented in the drill pages.

Suggestions for resource page use:
- Reproduce the resource pages and distribute to students for guidance when solving problems.
- Enlarge example problems and display them while teaching. (Alternately, post them on a bulletin board, at a work station, or in another visible area.)
- Make a transparency of problems for display on an overhead projector. Use erasable markers to review the steps for solving problems.

Included in the back of this book are removable flash cards ideal for individual review, group solving sessions, or as part of timed, sequential, or grouping activities. Carefully pull out the flash cards and cut them apart using scissors or a paper cutter.

## Finding Greatest Common Factor

To find the Greatest Common Factor (GCF), list all of the factors of the numbers. The factors that are the same between the numbers are the **common factors**. The number that is the highest among the common factors is the **greatest common factor**.

Example: Find the GCF for the numbers 15 and 30.

Factors of 15—1, 3, 5, (15)
Factors of 30—1, 2, 3, 5, 6, 10, (15), 30 } 1, 3, 5, and 15 are the common factors between 15 and 30. 15 is the greatest common factor.

## Finding Least Common Multiple

The least common multiple (LCM) is the lowest number that 2 or more different numbers can be divided into evenly.

Example: Find the LCM among the numbers 2, 3, and 4.

Multiples of 2—2, 4, 6, 8, 10, (12)
Multiples of 3—3, 6, 9, (12)
Multiples of 4—4, 8, (12) } 12 is the least common multiple.

## Fractions—Changing Fractions to Simplest Form

| Change $\frac{15}{20}$ to simplest form. | Divide 15 and 20 by their greatest common factor, 5. | $\frac{15 \div 5}{20 \div 5} = \frac{3}{4}$ | $\frac{3}{4}$ is the simplest form for $\frac{15}{20}$ because 3 and 4 have no factors in common other than 1. |

# Fractions—Changing Fractions to Mixed Numbers

| Change $\frac{10}{7}$ to simplest form. | A fraction can be changed to a mixed number when it names a number greater than 1. This is called an improper fraction. |

1. Divide 10 by 7.

$$7\overline{)10} \quad \begin{array}{r} 1\ R3 \\ \hline \end{array}$$
$$\underline{-\ 7}$$
$$3$$

2. Since 7 goes into 10 once, the whole number will be 1. Since there is a remainder of 3, the remaining fraction is $\frac{3}{7}$. Therefore the mixed number for $\frac{10}{7}$ is $1\frac{3}{7}$.

# Fractions—Changing Mixed Numbers to Improper Fractions

| Change $3\frac{1}{4}$ to simplest form. |

1. Multiply the whole number, 3, by the denominator, 4.

$$3 \times 4 = 12$$

2. Add the numerator, 1, to 12.

$$12 + 1 = 13$$

3. 13 is now the new numerator. The denominator, 4, remains the same. Therefore the improper fraction for $3\frac{1}{4}$ is $\frac{13}{4}$.

# Fractions—Multiplying Fractions

| Solve. $\frac{2}{3} \times \frac{3}{5}$ |

To multiply fractions, multiply the numerators, then multiply the denominators. Change to simplest form.

$$\frac{2}{3} \times \frac{3}{5} = \frac{2 \times 3 = 6}{3 \times 5 = 15} \quad \text{Therefore} \quad \frac{2}{3} \times \frac{3}{5} = \frac{6}{15}$$

# Fractions—Multiplying Whole Numbers and Fractions

| Solve. $3 \times \frac{1}{4}$ |

1. Rename the whole number as a fraction.

$$3 = \frac{3}{1}$$

2. Multiply the fractions.

$$\frac{3 \times 1 = 3}{1 \times 4 = 4}$$

# Fractions—Adding Fractions

| Solve. $\frac{3}{4} + \frac{2}{3}$ |

1. Rename the fractions so each has the same denominator.

$$\frac{3}{4} = \frac{9}{12} \quad \text{and} \quad \frac{2}{3} = \frac{8}{12}$$

2. Add the fractions that have been renamed.

$$\frac{9}{12} + \frac{8}{12} = \frac{17}{12}$$

3. Change to simplest form.

$$\frac{17}{12} = 1\frac{5}{12}$$

# Fractions—Subtracting Fractions with the Same Denominators

| Solve. $\frac{5}{6} - \frac{1}{6}$ |

1. Subtract the numerators and keep the denominators the same.

$$\frac{5 - 1}{6} = \frac{4}{6}$$

2. Change to simplest form when possible.

$$\frac{4}{6} = \frac{2}{3}$$

# Fractions—Subtracting Fractions from Whole Numbers

| Solve. $8 - \frac{4}{5}$ |

1. Rename the whole number so it is a fraction.

$$8 = \frac{8}{1}$$

2. Rename the fractions so they have the same denominator.

$$\frac{8}{1} - \frac{4}{5} = \frac{40}{5} - \frac{4}{5}$$

3. Subtract the fractions and change to simplest form.

$$\frac{40}{5} - \frac{4}{5} = \frac{36}{5} = 7\frac{1}{5}$$

## Fractions—Subtracting Fractions with Different Denominators

| Solve. |
|---|
| $\frac{4}{5} - \frac{2}{3}$ |

1. Rename the fractions so they both have the same denominator.

$$\frac{4}{5} - \frac{2}{3} = \frac{12}{15} - \frac{10}{15}$$

2. Subtract the renamed fractions.

$$\frac{12}{15} - \frac{10}{15} = \frac{2}{15}$$

## Fractions—Dividing Fractions

| Solve. |
|---|
| $\frac{1}{4} \div \frac{1}{2}$ |

| Solve. |
|---|
| $8 \div \frac{1}{3}$ |

1. Multiply the dividend by the reciprocal of the divisor.

$$\frac{1}{4} \times \frac{2}{1} = \frac{2}{1}$$

$$\frac{8}{1} \times \frac{3}{1} = \frac{24}{1}$$

2. Simplify the fraction when possible.

$$\frac{2}{1} = 2$$

$$\frac{24}{1} = 24$$

The multiplicative reciprocal of a number is 1 divided by the number. For example, the reciprocal of $\frac{1}{2}$ is $\frac{2}{1}$.

## Decimals—Adding & Subtracting Decimals

| Solve. |
|---|
| $54.03 + 3.2 =$ |

1. Line up the decimals and add or subtract as usual.

```
  54.03
+  3.20
------
  57.23
```

## Decimals—Multiplying Decimals

| Solve. |
|---|
| $.42 \times 5.6 =$ |

1. Multiply as usual.

```
   .42
 x 5.6
------
  2352
```

2. Count the number of digits after each decimal point in the problem and place a decimal point the same number of spaces to the left in the answer.

.4 2 ⟶ 2 digits after the decimal point
x 5.6 ⟶ 1 digit after the decimal point
2.352 ⟶ Move the decimal point three spaces to the left.

## Decimals—Dividing Decimals

| Solve. |
|---|
| $.06\overline{)5.412}$ |

1. Count the number of digits to the right of the decimal point in the divisor.

.06 ⟶ 2 digits are to the right of the decimal.

2. Move the decimal point in the dividend to the right as many spaces as you counted in the divisor.

$$\overline{)5.41.2}$$

3. Divide as usual.

```
     9 0 2
6)5 4 1 . 2
 -5 4
 ----
   0 1 2
  -1 2
  ----
     0
```

4. Bring up the decimal point.

```
     9 0 . 2
6)5 4 1 . 2
 -5 4
 ----
   0 1 2
  -1 2
  ----
     0
```

## Finding Percentages

| Solve. | Change the percentage number to a decimal and multiply times the whole number. | $20\% \text{ of } 80 = \underline{\hspace{1cm}}$ |
| --- | --- | --- |
| $20\% \text{ of } 80 = \underline{\hspace{1cm}}$ | | $.20 \times 80 = 16$ |

| Solve. | Rewrite the problem in the form of an equation and solve. | 1. $19 \text{ is } \underline{\hspace{0.5cm}}\% \text{ of } 95$  4. $19 = \frac{95n}{100}$ |
| --- | --- | --- |
| $19 \text{ is } \underline{\hspace{0.5cm}}\% \text{ of } 95$ | | 2. $19 = n\% \times 95$  5. $1{,}900 = 95x$<br>3. $19 = \frac{n}{100} \times 95$  6. $x = 20$ |

| Solve. | Rewrite the problem in the form of an equation and solve. | 1. $24 \text{ is } 60\% \text{ of } \underline{\hspace{0.8cm}}$  4. $2{,}400 = 60n$ |
| --- | --- | --- |
| $24 \text{ is } 60\% \text{ of } \underline{\hspace{0.8cm}}$ | | 2. $24 = \frac{60}{100} \times n$  5. $n = 40$<br>3. $24 = \frac{60n}{100}$ |

| Solve. | Rewrite the problem in the form of an equation and solve. | 1. $\underline{\hspace{0.8cm}} \text{ is } 40\% \text{ of } 30$  4. $n = 1\frac{1}{5}$ |
| --- | --- | --- |
| $\underline{\hspace{0.8cm}} \text{ is } 40\% \text{ of } 30$ | | 2. $n = \frac{40}{100} \times 30$<br>3. $n = \frac{120}{100}$ |

## Order of Operations

| Solve. | The order of solving operations is as follows: | $(3 + 2) \times (7 - 1) =$ |
| --- | --- | --- |
| $(3 + 2) \times (7 - 1)$ | 1. Calculate all math in parentheses.<br>2. Multiply and divide from left to right.<br>3. Add and subtract from left to right. | $5 \times (7 - 1) =$<br>$5 \times 6 =$<br>$30$ |

## Integers

Integers include all whole numbers, both positive and negative, and the number zero.

## Adding Integers

When addends have the **same sign**, add them.

    If they are both positive, the answer remains positive.

    If they are both negative, the answer is negative.

        Examples: $3 + 6 = 9$     $^-3 + {}^-6 = {}^-9$

When addends have **different signs**, subtract the numbers and use the sign of the greater addend.      Examples: $^-8 + {}^+3 = {}^-5$     $^+15 + {}^-6 = 9$     $^-4 + {}^+7 = 3$     $^+3 + {}^-10 = {}^-7$

## Subtracting Integers

To subtract integers, add the opposite of the number being subtracted.

        Examples:    $8 - 3 = 8 + {}^-3 = 5$        $8 - {}^-3 = 8 + 3 = 11$

# Multiplying Integers

To multiply positive and negative integers, remember the following rules:
- A positive times a positive equals a positive.
- A positive times a negative equals a negative.
- A negative times a negative equals a positive.

Examples:

$$3 \times 4 = 12$$
$$3 \times -4 = -12$$
$$-3 \times 4 = -12$$
$$-3 \times -4 = 12$$

# Evaluating Expressions

| Solve. |
| --- |
| If a = 4 then |
| a + 6 = _____ |

Substitute the value given for the variable and add as usual.

$$a + 6 = 4 + 6 = 10$$

When evaluating an expression where the value of the variable is unknown, isolate the variable on one side of the equation to find its value. Keep in mind that if you add, subtract, multiply, or divide on one side of the equation, you must do the same on the other side. If you perform an operation on only one side of the equation, then both sides of the equation are no longer equal.

| Find the value of x. |
| --- |
| 5 + x = 8 |

Isolate the variable, x, on one side of the equation. To do this, subtract 5 from each side of the equation.

$$5 (- 5) + x = 8 (- 5) \qquad x = 3$$

| Find the value of y. |
| --- |
| y - 4 = 25 |

Isolate the variable, y, on one side of the equation. To do this, add 4 to each side of the equation.

$$y - 4 (+ 4) = 25 (+ 4) \qquad y = 29$$

| Find the value of r. |
| --- |
| 4r = 20 |

Isolate the variable, r, on one side of the equation. To do this, divide both sides of the equation by 4.

$$\frac{4r}{(4)} = \frac{20}{(4)} \qquad r = 5$$

| Find the value of a. |
| --- |
| 2a - 20 = 10 |

1. Add 20 to both sides of the equation.

$$2a - 20 (+ 20) = 10 (+ 20) \qquad 2a = 30$$

2. Divide both sides of the equation by 2.

$$\frac{2a}{(2)} = \frac{30}{(2)} \qquad a = 15$$

## Calculating Exponents

To calculate a number to a certain power, multiply the root number by itself the number of times indicated by the power.

Example:

$2^2 = 2 \times 2 = 4$

$2^3 = 2 \times 2 \times 2 = 8$

$2^4 = 2 \times 2 \times 2 \times 2 = 16$

$2^5 = 2 \times 2 \times 2 \times 2 \times 2 = 32$

$2^6 = 2 \times 2 \times 2 \times 2 \times 2 \times 2 = 64$

## Finding Square Roots

The square root of a number is a factor of a number that, when multiplied by itself, equals that number.

Example:

$N = 16$

Find the square root of 16.

The square root of 16 is 4 because $4 \times 4 = 16$.

Study the chart below.

| n | $\sqrt{n}$ | n | $\sqrt{n}$ | n | $\sqrt{n}$ | n | $\sqrt{n}$ |
|---|---|---|---|---|---|---|---|
| 1 | 1 | 121 | 11 | 441 | 21 | 961 | 31 |
| 4 | 2 | 144 | 12 | 484 | 22 | 1,024 | 32 |
| 9 | 3 | 169 | 13 | 529 | 23 | 1,089 | 33 |
| 16 | 4 | 196 | 14 | 576 | 24 | 1,156 | 34 |
| 25 | 5 | 225 | 15 | 625 | 25 | 1,225 | 35 |
| 36 | 6 | 256 | 16 | 676 | 26 | 1,296 | 36 |
| 49 | 7 | 289 | 17 | 729 | 27 | 1,369 | 37 |
| 64 | 8 | 324 | 18 | 784 | 28 | 1,444 | 38 |
| 81 | 9 | 361 | 19 | 841 | 29 | 1,521 | 39 |
| 100 | 10 | 400 | 20 | 900 | 30 | 1,600 | 40 |

Multiply.

1.
```
  423
x   6
 2538
```

2.
```
  872
x   9
 7238
```

3.
```
  584
x   2
 1168
```

4.
```
  675
x   5
 3405
```

5.
```
  862
x   4
 3448
```

6.
```
  905
x   8
 7240
```

7.
```
  782
x   3
 2346
```

8.
```
  652
x   4
 2608
```

9.
```
   483
x   21
  1483
+ 966
 10143
```

10.
```
   985
x   52
  1970
+ 4925
 11220
```

11.
```
  125
x  10
  000
 1250
```

12.
```
   863
x   49
  7767
+ 3452 0
  42287
```

13.
```
  187
x  28
 1496
+374 0
 5236
```

14.
```
   229
x   15
  1145
+ 2290
  3435
```

15.
```
   697
x   54
  2488
+ 34556
  37638
```

16.
```
  754
x  13
 2262
+7540
 9802
```

17.
```
   237
x   95
  1185
+ 21330
  22515
```

18.
```
   863
x   42
  1926
+ 34920
  36346
```

19.
```
  307
x  72
```

20.
```
  428
```

Name_____

Multiply.

1.  835
    x 52

2.  298
    x 42

3.  785
    x 54

4.  962
    x 16

5.  741
    x 28

6.  284
    x 625

7.  103
    x 294

8.  786
    x 528

9.  642
    x 310

10. 925
    x 652

11. 107
    x 643

12. 822
    x 467

13. 483
    x 425

14. 819
    x 652

15. 407
    x 300

16. 925
    x 462

17. 117
    x 563

18. 628
    x 413

19. 217
    x 648

20. 394
    x 225

**Total Problems  20   Problems Correct ____**

Name_____     Skill: Multiplying Two, Three, and
                                          Four Digit Numbers

Multiply.

1.  1,248        2.  9,071        3.  8,265        4.  3,542        5.  2,331
    x   73           x   51           x   49           x   28           x   78


6.  4,918        7.  7,510        8.  8,162        9.  4,076       10. 9,651
    x   56           x   50           x   35           x  328           x  525


11. 8,600       12. 2,542       13. 1,359       14. 4,077       15. 3,007
    x  315           x  647           x  689           x  178           x  848


16. 5,215       17. 4,252       18. 6,594       19. 3,103       20. 4,255
    x  781           x  843           x  122           x  212           x  382


Total Problems  20   Problems Correct ____

3

Name_____ Skill: Dividing by One Digit Numbers

Divide.

1.  9|42

2.  5|64

3.  4|38

4.  7|21

5.  3|24

6.  5|62

7.  9|45

8.  6|36

9.  5|58

10. 6|87

11. 3|78

12. 9|28

13. 7|65

14. 3|43

15. 9|35

20×3=60
23×3=69
26×3=78

9×3=27

16. 6|51

17. 8|82

18. 6|94

19. 5|57

20. 2|25

21. 4|18

22. 8|33

23. 5|25

24. 7|36

25. 8|93

Name_____     Skill: Dividing by One and Two
                                          Digit Numbers

Divide.

1.
5⟌425

2.
8⟌325

3.
3⟌672

4.
6⟌453

5.
4⟌681

6.
9⟌553

7.
7⟌957

8.
5⟌496

9.
2⟌5,090

10.
38⟌7,231

11.
32⟌4,852

12.
26⟌2,569

13.
3⟌1,542

14.
2⟌5,128

15.
7⟌3,182

16.
5⟌7,825

17.
4⟌9,760

18.
7⟌4,027

19
4⟌6,011

20.
6⟌8,304

**Total Problems __20__  Problems Correct ____**

5

Divide.

1. 25)467        2. 56)306        3. 61)162        4. 45)671

5. 63)339        6. 97)927        7. 77)183        8. 82)783

9. 89)298        10. 76)8,011     11. 36)2,470     12. 51)3,520

13. 38)1,784     14. 85)4,240     15. 72)5,621     16. 97)3,876

17. 91)8,847     18. 55)7,562     19. 68)2,513     20. 24)6,628

Total Problems _20_  Problems Correct _____

Divide.

1. 21 | 1,247     2. 51 | 4,320     3. 42 | 5,794     4. 35 | 2,395

5. 75 | 5,321     6. 67 | 3,072     7. 52 | 7,894     8. 86 | 6,190

9. 49 | 3,437     10. 83 | 6,235     11. 22 | 1,384     12. 47 | 4,718

13. 56 | 2,357     14. 34 | 8,532     15. 99 | 4,796     16. 73 | 5,060

17. 68 | 9,949     18. 71 | 3,218     19. 26 | 7,198     20. 37 | 6,217

Total Problems __20__ Problems Correct ____

Name _Aaron_      Skill: Changing Fractions to Simplest Form

Change each fraction or mixed number to simplest form.

1. $\dfrac{20}{25} =$    $\dfrac{4}{5}$

2. $\dfrac{50}{70} =$    $\dfrac{5}{7}$

3. $\dfrac{25}{35} =$    $\dfrac{5}{7}$

4. $\dfrac{32}{64} =$    $\dfrac{4}{8} = \dfrac{1}{2}$

5. $\dfrac{10}{25} =$    $\dfrac{2}{5}$

6. $\dfrac{7}{49} =$    $\dfrac{1}{7}$

7. $\dfrac{35}{42} =$    $\dfrac{5}{6}$

8. $\dfrac{12}{18} =$    $\dfrac{2}{3}$

9. $\dfrac{19}{38} =$    $\dfrac{1}{2}$

10. $\dfrac{56}{63} =$

11. $\dfrac{32}{80} =$    $\dfrac{4}{10}\ \dfrac{2}{5}$

12. $\dfrac{49}{56} =$    $\dfrac{7}{8}$

13. $\dfrac{27}{36} =$    $\dfrac{3}{4}$

14. $\dfrac{12}{20} =$    $\dfrac{3}{5}$

15. $\dfrac{30}{42} =$    $\dfrac{5}{7} = \dfrac{15}{21}$

16. $2\dfrac{16}{36} =$    $\dfrac{4}{9}$

17. $3\dfrac{25}{60} =$    $\dfrac{5}{12}$

18. $1\dfrac{10}{20} =$    $\dfrac{2}{4}\ \dfrac{1}{2}$

19. $4\dfrac{4}{40} =$    $\dfrac{1}{10}$

20. $4\dfrac{24}{30} =$    $\dfrac{8}{10}\ \dfrac{4}{5}$

21. $3\dfrac{10}{15} =$    $\dfrac{2}{3}$

22. $3\dfrac{3}{9} =$    $\dfrac{1}{3}$

23. $8\dfrac{8}{16} =$    $\dfrac{2}{4}\ \dfrac{1}{2}$

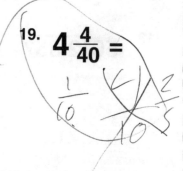

**Total Problems 23 Problems Correct 23**

8

Name_____ Skill: Changing Fractions to Simplest Form

Change each fraction or mixed number to simplest form.

1.  $\dfrac{25}{50} =$     2.  $\dfrac{35}{75} =$     3.  $\dfrac{15}{25} =$     4.  $\dfrac{16}{18} =$     5.  $\dfrac{32}{60} =$

6.  $\dfrac{5}{20} =$     7.  $\dfrac{9}{81} =$     8.  $\dfrac{50}{60} =$     9.  $\dfrac{55}{75} =$     10.  $\dfrac{42}{49} =$

11.  $\dfrac{12}{36} =$     12.  $\dfrac{48}{52} =$     13.  $\dfrac{93}{663} =$     14.  $\dfrac{45}{81} =$     15.  $\dfrac{21}{28} =$

16.  $6\dfrac{35}{70} =$     17.  $9\dfrac{45}{60} =$     18.  $4\dfrac{28}{56} =$     19.  $5\dfrac{2}{92} =$

20.  $3\dfrac{2}{8} =$     21.  $7\dfrac{24}{36} =$     22.  $8\dfrac{9}{9} =$     23.  $5\dfrac{9}{27} =$

Total Problems __23__ Problems Correct _____

Name_____

Skill: Changing Improper Fractions
to Mixed Numbers

Change each fraction to a mixed number.

1. $\frac{36}{24} =$

2. $\frac{90}{36} =$

3. $\frac{48}{42} =$

4. $\frac{50}{15} =$

5. $\frac{19}{12} =$

6. $\frac{50}{41} =$

7. $\frac{9}{6} =$

8. $\frac{47}{16} =$

9. $\frac{55}{13} =$

10. $\frac{62}{27} =$

11. $\frac{41}{33} =$

12. $\frac{48}{36} =$

13. $\frac{23}{13} =$

14. $\frac{57}{28} =$

15. $\frac{23}{18} =$

16. $\frac{98}{45} =$

17. $\frac{76}{36} =$

18. $\frac{16}{13} =$

19. $\frac{45}{21} =$

20. $\frac{21}{15} =$

21. $\frac{12}{11} =$

22. $\frac{92}{52} =$

23. $\frac{85}{36} =$

24. $\frac{92}{81} =$

25. $\frac{38}{37} =$

**Total Problems _25_ Problems Correct ____**

Change each mixed number to a fraction.

1. $1\frac{2}{5} =$    2. $3\frac{5}{6} =$    3. $9\frac{2}{7} =$

4. $6\frac{1}{5} =$    5. $6\frac{1}{4} =$    6. $7\frac{1}{2} =$

7. $2\frac{1}{8} =$    8. $9\frac{2}{3} =$    9. $1\frac{3}{5} =$

10. $4\frac{1}{7} =$    11. $4\frac{5}{8} =$    12. $5\frac{3}{8} =$

**Total Problems  12  Problems Correct ____**

Multiply. Write answers in simplest form.

1.  $\dfrac{1}{4} \times \dfrac{2}{5} =$

2.  $\dfrac{1}{2} \times \dfrac{7}{8} =$

3.  $\dfrac{3}{8} \times \dfrac{2}{9} =$

4.  $\dfrac{1}{5} \times \dfrac{5}{6} =$

5.  $\dfrac{3}{5} \times \dfrac{5}{8} =$

6.  $\dfrac{9}{10} \times \dfrac{3}{7} =$

7.  $\dfrac{2}{3} \times \dfrac{3}{4} =$

8.  $\dfrac{1}{7} \times \dfrac{3}{5} =$

9.  $\dfrac{5}{8} \times \dfrac{1}{6} =$

10.  $\dfrac{1}{3} \times \dfrac{1}{9} =$

11.  $\dfrac{2}{9} \times \dfrac{1}{8} =$

12.  $\dfrac{7}{8} \times \dfrac{1}{4} =$

13.  $\dfrac{3}{4} \times \dfrac{7}{8} =$

14.  $\dfrac{2}{3} \times \dfrac{5}{9} =$

15.  $\dfrac{1}{4} \times \dfrac{3}{4} =$

**Total Problems  15   Problems Correct ____**

Name_____   Skill:  Multiplying Fractions

Multiply. Write answers in simplest form.

1. $\frac{1}{7} \times \frac{1}{2} =$

2. $\frac{3}{4} \times \frac{5}{7} =$

3. $\frac{2}{9} \times \frac{3}{5} =$

4. $\frac{2}{5} \times \frac{2}{5} =$

5. $\frac{3}{8} \times \frac{1}{2} =$

6. $\frac{4}{5} \times \frac{3}{6} =$

7. $\frac{3}{5} \times \frac{1}{6} =$

8. $\frac{5}{7} \times \frac{2}{9} =$

9. $\frac{8}{9} \times \frac{6}{7} =$

10. $\frac{2}{5} \times \frac{4}{7} =$

11. $\frac{3}{6} \times \frac{7}{8} =$

12. $\frac{5}{6} \times \frac{1}{3} =$

13. $\frac{5}{9} \times \frac{4}{8} =$

14. $\frac{3}{7} \times \frac{1}{5} =$

15. $\frac{1}{3} \times \frac{1}{5} =$

**Total Problems  15   Problems Correct ____**

Multiply. Write answers in simplest form.

1. $9 \times 3\frac{1}{3} =$          2. $8 \times 1\frac{1}{8} =$          3. $6 \times 1\frac{4}{9} =$

4. $3 \times 5\frac{1}{5} =$          5. $6 \times 3\frac{1}{6} =$          6. $7 \times 2\frac{3}{5} =$

7. $9 \times 4\frac{3}{5} =$          8. $7 \times 2\frac{5}{6} =$          9. $2 \times 1\frac{1}{2} =$

10. $1 \times 8\frac{1}{12} =$          11. $4 \times 8\frac{1}{3} =$          12. $6 \times 2\frac{1}{5} =$

**Total Problems  12   Problems Correct ____**

Multiply. Write answers in simplest form.

1. $3\frac{1}{3} \times 9\frac{1}{2} =$

2. $8\frac{1}{6} \times 2\frac{3}{5} =$

3. $9\frac{2}{7} \times 4\frac{1}{5} =$

4. $4\frac{1}{5} \times 5\frac{1}{2} =$

5. $5\frac{2}{5} \times 4\frac{4}{9} =$

6. $5\frac{1}{8} \times 8\frac{1}{3} =$

7. $1\frac{3}{7} \times 4\frac{3}{4} =$

8. $2\frac{6}{7} \times 5\frac{1}{4} =$

9. $4\frac{5}{8} \times 8\frac{2}{7} =$

10. $1\frac{3}{4} \times 8\frac{3}{4} =$

11. $3\frac{2}{3} \times 1\frac{3}{8} =$

12. $8\frac{4}{9} \times 2\frac{5}{6} =$

Total Problems __12__ Problems Correct ____

Name_____

Divide. Write answers in simplest form.

1.  $\dfrac{1}{2} \div \dfrac{3}{4} =$

2.  $\dfrac{5}{16} \div \dfrac{5}{8} =$

3.  $\dfrac{8}{9} \div \dfrac{14}{15} =$

4.  $\dfrac{3}{4} \div \dfrac{13}{16} =$

5.  $\dfrac{3}{4} \div \dfrac{1}{2} =$

6.  $\dfrac{3}{5} \div \dfrac{3}{12} =$

7.  $\dfrac{8}{15} \div \dfrac{4}{5} =$

8.  $\dfrac{4}{5} \div \dfrac{4}{7} =$

9.  $\dfrac{4}{10} \div \dfrac{15}{27} =$

10. $\dfrac{3}{4} \div \dfrac{1}{8} =$

11. $\dfrac{5}{10} \div \dfrac{12}{25} =$

12. $\dfrac{21}{40} \div \dfrac{7}{24} =$

13. $\dfrac{25}{38} \div \dfrac{15}{32} =$

14. $\dfrac{7}{8} \div \dfrac{1}{2} =$

15. $\dfrac{7}{12} \div \dfrac{14}{28} =$

Total Problems __15__ Problems Correct ____

Divide. Write answers in simplest form.

1. $\dfrac{7}{50} \div \dfrac{21}{35} =$

2. $\dfrac{7}{12} \div \dfrac{5}{6} =$

3. $\dfrac{3}{4} \div \dfrac{27}{36} =$

4. $\dfrac{1}{2} \div \dfrac{4}{9} =$

5. $\dfrac{7}{10} \div \dfrac{1}{6} =$

6. $\dfrac{7}{12} \div \dfrac{14}{15} =$

7. $\dfrac{7}{12} \div \dfrac{1}{2} =$

8. $\dfrac{2}{3} \div \dfrac{8}{9} =$

9. $\dfrac{1}{10} \div \dfrac{15}{30} =$

10. $\dfrac{1}{7} \div \dfrac{1}{3} =$

11. $\dfrac{5}{10} \div \dfrac{12}{25} =$

12. $\dfrac{18}{33} \div \dfrac{6}{11} =$

13. $\dfrac{25}{36} \div \dfrac{5}{27} =$

14. $\dfrac{1}{6} \div \dfrac{1}{3} =$

15. $\dfrac{7}{12} \div \dfrac{5}{6} =$

**Total Problems  15   Problems Correct ____**

Divide. Write answers in simplest form.

1. $2 \div 1\frac{1}{2} =$

2. $9 \div 3\frac{1}{3} =$

3. $2 \div 2\frac{1}{4} =$

4. $6 \div 4\frac{5}{6} =$

5. $7 \div 7\frac{3}{4} =$

6. $6 \div 6\frac{1}{9} =$

7. $5 \div 3\frac{2}{5} =$

8. $11 \div 5\frac{7}{8} =$

9. $9 \div 2\frac{5}{6} =$

10. $4 \div 4\frac{4}{5} =$

11. $2 \div 5\frac{3}{5} =$

12. $3 \div 4\frac{1}{6} =$

13. $6 \div 2\frac{1}{2} =$

14. $4 \div 1\frac{1}{4} =$

15. $8 \div 4\frac{1}{2} =$

**Total Problems  15   Problems Correct ____**

18

Name_____

Skill: Dividing Mixed Numbers by Mixed Numbers

Divide. Write answers in simplest form.

1. $1\frac{1}{2} \div 2\frac{2}{3} =$

2. $4\frac{2}{3} \div 1\frac{7}{9} =$

3. $1\frac{5}{6} \div 2\frac{2}{3} =$

4. $5\frac{1}{4} \div 1\frac{1}{8} =$

5. $5\frac{1}{7} \div 5\frac{1}{3} =$

6. $4\frac{2}{7} \div 5\frac{1}{4} =$

7. $2\frac{1}{7} \div 8\frac{4}{7} =$

8. $4\frac{2}{7} \div 1\frac{1}{5} =$

9. $5\frac{3}{5} \div 2\frac{2}{5} =$

10. $9\frac{1}{6} \div 8\frac{1}{4} =$

11. $3\frac{1}{4} \div 1\frac{7}{8} =$

12. $4\frac{4}{9} \div 6\frac{2}{3} =$

Total Problems __12__  Problems Correct ____

19

Name_____     Skill:  Finding the Greatest Common Factor

List the factors for each pair of numbers and find the greatest common factor.

| | | Factors | Greatest Common Factor |
|---|---|---|---|
| 1. | 27, 36 | | |
| 2. | 42, 49 | | |
| 3. | 15, 18 | | |
| 4. | 16, 24 | | |
| 5. | 20, 40 | | |
| 6. | 63, 81 | | |
| 7. | 25, 50 | | |
| 8. | 36, 48 | | |
| 9. | 44, 66 | | |
| 10. | 22, 33 | | |

Total Problems __10__  Problems Correct ____

Name_____ Skill: Finding the Greatest Common Factor

Find the greatest common factor for each set of numbers.

1. **72, 90** _____

2. **24, 32** _____

3. **15, 30** _____

4. **36, 27** _____

5. **52, 32** _____

6. **36, 81** _____

7. **50, 20** _____

8. **16, 20** _____

9. **24, 46** _____

10. **48, 56** _____

11. **42, 81, 51** _____

12. **18, 21, 9** _____

13. **24, 16, 32** _____

14. **49, 28, 21** _____

**Total Problems __14__ Problems Correct ____**

21

Name_____     Skill:  Finding the Least Common Multiple

Find the least common multiple of each pair of numbers.

1. **3, 5** _____          2. **5, 10** _____

3. **4, 3** _____          4. **2, 10** _____

5. **8, 12** _____          6. **9, 12** _____

7. **7, 8** _____          8. **6, 9** _____

9. **7, 4** _____          10. **11, 10** _____

11. **15, 25** _____          12. **8, 3** _____

13. **5, 7** _____          14. **9, 3** _____

**Total Problems  14   Problems Correct ____**

Name_____ Skill: Finding the Least Common Multiple

Find the least common multiple of each set of numbers.

1. **2, 4** _____

2. **8, 3** _____

3. **5, 3** _____

4. **6, 9** _____

5. **12, 24** _____

6. **20, 30** _____

7. **8, 4** _____

8. **12, 18** _____

9. **10, 15** _____

10. **6, 10** _____

11. **9, 8, 12** _____

12. **7, 9** _____

13. **2, 7, 14** _____

14. **15, 30** _____

**Total Problems _14_ Problems Correct ____**

Name_____

Add. Write answers in simplest form.

1. $\dfrac{1}{4} + \dfrac{3}{5} =$      2. $\dfrac{1}{2} + \dfrac{2}{3} =$      3. $\dfrac{7}{8} + \dfrac{5}{6} =$

4. $\dfrac{3}{4} + \dfrac{2}{7} =$      5. $\dfrac{2}{7} + \dfrac{5}{14} =$      6. $\dfrac{7}{8} + \dfrac{1}{7} =$

7. $\dfrac{7}{9} + \dfrac{3}{3} =$      8. $\dfrac{1}{3} + \dfrac{3}{8} =$      9. $\dfrac{5}{8} + \dfrac{1}{6} =$

10. $\dfrac{1}{7} + \dfrac{2}{9} =$      11. $\dfrac{2}{6} + \dfrac{1}{8} =$      12. $\dfrac{3}{7} + \dfrac{1}{4} =$

13. $\dfrac{5}{9} + \dfrac{7}{8} =$      14. $\dfrac{1}{6} + \dfrac{5}{8} =$      15. $\dfrac{5}{8} + \dfrac{3}{7} =$

**Total Problems** __15__ **Problems Correct** ____

Name_____          Skill: Adding Fractions

Add. Write answers in simplest form.

1. $\dfrac{1}{3} + \dfrac{2}{3} =$

2. $\dfrac{5}{6} + \dfrac{1}{3} =$

3. $\dfrac{4}{5} + \dfrac{1}{3} =$

4. $\dfrac{3}{5} + \dfrac{1}{4} =$

5. $\dfrac{3}{8} + \dfrac{5}{16} =$

6. $\dfrac{2}{5} + \dfrac{1}{2} =$

7. $\dfrac{5}{6} + \dfrac{1}{3} =$

8. $\dfrac{1}{2} + \dfrac{2}{7} =$

9. $\dfrac{5}{6} + \dfrac{1}{5} =$

10. $\dfrac{1}{6} + \dfrac{2}{3} =$

11. $\dfrac{2}{7} + \dfrac{1}{2} =$

12. $\dfrac{5}{6} + \dfrac{1}{3} =$

13. $\dfrac{1}{6} + \dfrac{1}{8} =$

14. $\dfrac{4}{9} + \dfrac{3}{8} =$

15. $\dfrac{2}{3} + \dfrac{2}{5} =$

Total Problems __15__ Problems Correct ____

25

Name_____

Subtract. Write answers in simplest form.

1. $\dfrac{4}{5} - \dfrac{3}{5} =$

2. $\dfrac{3}{6} - \dfrac{1}{6} =$

3. $\dfrac{4}{5} - \dfrac{2}{5} =$

4. $\dfrac{3}{5} - \dfrac{1}{5} =$

5. $\dfrac{5}{16} - \dfrac{2}{16} =$

6. $\dfrac{2}{8} - \dfrac{1}{8} =$

7. $\dfrac{5}{6} - \dfrac{1}{6} =$

8. $\dfrac{7}{9} - \dfrac{2}{9} =$

9. $\dfrac{1}{8} - \dfrac{1}{8} =$

10. $\dfrac{3}{4} - \dfrac{2}{4} =$

11. $\dfrac{5}{7} - \dfrac{1}{7} =$

12. $\dfrac{2}{2} - \dfrac{1}{2} =$

13. $\dfrac{1}{3} - \dfrac{1}{3} =$

14. $\dfrac{4}{9} - \dfrac{3}{9} =$

15. $\dfrac{3}{5} - \dfrac{2}{5} =$

Total Problems _15_ Problems Correct ____

Name_____

Subtract. Write answers in simplest form.

1.
$2$
$- \dfrac{7}{8}$

2.
$4$
$- \dfrac{2}{5}$

3.
$5$
$- \dfrac{2}{3}$

4.
$6$
$- \dfrac{1}{8}$

5.
$3$
$- \dfrac{3}{4}$

6.
$8$
$- \dfrac{9}{10}$

7.
$7$
$- \dfrac{4}{5}$

8.
$4$
$- \dfrac{3}{10}$

9.
$5$
$- \dfrac{6}{9}$

10.
$4$
$- \dfrac{2}{6}$

11.
$5$
$- \dfrac{2}{5}$

12.
$10$
$- \dfrac{1}{2}$

13.
$12$
$- \dfrac{5}{7}$

14.
$9$
$- \dfrac{1}{3}$

15.
$4$
$- \dfrac{7}{8}$

16.
$3$
$- \dfrac{6}{7}$

**Total Problems   16   Problems Correct _____**

Name_____

Subtract. Write answers in simplest form.

1. 
$$15\frac{3}{8}$$
$$-\ \ \frac{3}{8}$$

2.
$$10\frac{1}{2}$$
$$-\ \ \frac{2}{5}$$

3.
$$1$$
$$-\ \ \frac{1}{3}$$

4.
$$2$$
$$-\ \ \frac{6}{11}$$

5.
$$5$$
$$-\ \ \frac{3}{5}$$

6.
$$9$$
$$-\ \ \frac{3}{7}$$

7.
$$14$$
$$-\ \ \frac{2}{9}$$

8.
$$13$$
$$-\ \ \frac{2}{3}$$

9.
$$1$$
$$-\ \ \frac{7}{8}$$

10.
$$6$$
$$-\ \ \frac{1}{5}$$

11.
$$7$$
$$-\ \ \frac{5}{6}$$

12.
$$5$$
$$-\ \ \frac{1}{4}$$

13.
$$8$$
$$-\ \ \frac{3}{4}$$

14.
$$4$$
$$-\ \ \frac{1}{2}$$

15.
$$2\frac{1}{3}$$
$$-\ \ \frac{1}{6}$$

16.
$$6$$
$$-\ \ \frac{3}{7}$$

**Total Problems __16__ Problems Correct _____**

Name_____          Skill: Adding Decimals

Add.

| 1. | 5.6 <br> + 2.3 | 2. | 2.5 <br> + 8.6 | 3. | 11.5 <br> + 3.3 | 4. | 2.6 <br> + 7.8 |
|---|---|---|---|---|---|---|---|

| 5. | 21.5 <br> + 2.9 | 6. | 38.7 <br> + 3.4 | 7. | 94.5 <br> + 37.6 | 8. | 80.5 <br> + 35.3 |
|---|---|---|---|---|---|---|---|

| 9. | .54 <br> + .82 | 10. | 5.78 <br> + 5.07 | 11. | 32.52 <br> + 12.63 | 12. | 15.87 <br> + 77.19 |
|---|---|---|---|---|---|---|---|

13.  2.2
     1.5
   + 7.7

14.  41.7
      5.2
   + 2.4

15.  7.1
    18.5
  + 15.4

16.  10.12
     10.27
   + 90.33

17.  2.456
     3.088
   + 8.645

18.  57.00
     87.49
   + 37.12

19.  212.6
     422.3
   + 223.7

20.  4.022
     1.341
   + .037

**Total Problems _20_ Problems Correct _____**

29

Name_____                Skill: Adding Decimals

Add.

1.   3.35          2.   33.87          3.    .255          4.     .3
      .01               45.88              1.70                4.2
  + 4.60            + 1.12            + 23.15             + .22


5.  221.7          6.  317.5          7.   24.15          8.   1.88
      3.35               1.4                .15              22.03
  +     .07          + 88.4            + 5.67             + .09


9.   12.56        10.   5.14         11.    5.1          12.   4.5
     73.38               .027              7.80               5.4
   + .08            + 72.5            + 80.4             + 12.97


13. 12.7 + .13 + 1.2 =            14. .735 + 6.55 + 13 =


15. 31.5 + 1.2 + 571.35 =         16. 42 + .522 + 7.2 =


Total Problems  16  Problems Correct ____

30

Name_____

Add.

1. $1.429 + 21.8 =$

2. $.9 + .85 =$

3. $5.15 + 17.623 =$

4. $52.14 + 12.7 =$

5. $.911 + 3.2 =$

6. $46.25 + 12.56 =$

7. $1.654 + 2.511 =$

8. $1.23 + 1.654 =$

9. $81.75 + 23.55 =$

10. $7.521 + 2.1 =$

11. $21.2 + .231 =$

12. $68.58 + .925 =$

13. $16.68 + 23.665 =$

14. $1.522 + 8.2 =$

15. $88.17 + 26.5 =$

16. $3.901 + 39.01 =$

Total Problems __16__ Problems Correct ____

Name_____

Add.

1.  **12.4 + 2.689 =**

2.  **.006 + 1.4 =**

3.  **18.529 + 4.5 =**

4.  **23.09 + 16 =**

5.  **18.4 + .06 =**

6.  **.023 + 23.4 =**

7.  **3.49 + 8.9 =**

8.  **.024 + 73.5 =**

9.  **123.4 + 12.2 =**

10. **23.1 + 16.902 =**

11. **56.1 + 26.49 =**

12. **5.01 + 273.4 =**

13. **.007 + 8.32 =**

14. **17.829 + 2.2 =**

15. **.52 + .049 =**

16. **75.23 + 26.01 =**

**Total Problems _16_ Problems Correct ____**

Name_____     Skill: Subtracting Decimals

Subtract.

1.   .7
   − .2

2.   .8
   − .3

3.   .6
   − .2

4.   .9
   − .5

5.   .45
   − .21

6.   .77
   − .25

7.   .24
   − .15

8.   .50
   − .11

9.   .885
   − .325

10.   .987
   − .521

11.   .608
   − .321

12.   .952
   − .335

13.   19.6
   − 2.1

14.   22.6
   − .2

15.   71.6
   − .7

16.   39.99
   − 3.72

17.   80.15
   − .32

18.   95.33
   − 5.21

19.   88.43
   − 12.03

20.   61.91
   − 3.41

**Total Problems  20   Problems Correct _____**

Name_____

Subtract.

1.   15.867
   –  4.27

2.   30.322
   –  .51

3.   21.423
   – 1.2

4.   62.456
   –  4.2

5.   4.31
   – .4

6.   826.83
   – 22.5

7.   91.35
   –  2.672

8.   91.384
   – 2.788

9.   6.224
   – 3.04

10.  30.9
   –  5.21

11.  81.1
   –  2.652

12.  54.75
   –  6.213

13.  43.154 – 2.08 =

14.  .45 – .224 =

15.  .9 – .832 =

16.  3.3 – 1.657 =

Total Problems  16  Problems Correct ____

Name_____     Skill: Multiplying Decimals

Multiply.

1.    .2
  x 5

2.    .3
  x 6

3.    .4
  x .1

4.    .7
  x .8

5.    .09
  x 2

6.    .06
  x 5

7.    4
  x .12

8.    3
  x .25

9.    9.5
  x 3

10.    5.5
  x 2

11.    3.56
  x 6

12.    5.66
  x .8

13.    .22
  x .23

14.    7.8
  x 5.4

15.    .15
  x .21

16.    1.5
  x 3.1

17.    .86
  x 5.4

18.    4.1
  x 5.5

19.    .07
  x 12

20.    32
  x 5.4

**Total Problems  20   Problems Correct ____**

Name_____          Skill: Multiplying Decimals

Multiply.

1.   .231
   x 1.3

2.   6.42
   x 2.3

3.   7.41
   x .9

4.   5.11
   x .51

5.   .611
   x 110

6.   23.7
   x 13.5

7.   16.2
   x 34.7

8.   8.22
   x .852

9.   .888
   x .402

10.   325.5
   x 54.7

11.   78.45
   x 7.26

12.   3.365
   x .32

13.  27.556 x 85.4 =

14.  .623 x 5.07 =

15.  3.850 x 905.7 =

16.  55.4 x .657 =

Total Problems __16__  Problems Correct ____

Name_____  Skill: Multiplying Decimals

Multiply.

| 1. | .112 | 2. | 8.56 | 3. | 3.66 | 4. | 8.24 |
|---|---|---|---|---|---|---|---|
| | x 1.4 | | x 2.1 | | x .7 | | x .71 |

| 5. | 2.22 | 6. | 88.4 | 7. | 18.7 | 8. | 9.32 |
|---|---|---|---|---|---|---|---|
| | x 1.2 | | x 13.5 | | x 12.9 | | x .652 |

| 9. | .752 | 10. | 119.5 | 11. | 44.45 | 12. | 3.206 |
|---|---|---|---|---|---|---|---|
| | x .366 | | x 24.7 | | x 7.81 | | x .71 |

13. $37.899 \times 23.8 =$

14. $.611 \times 5.20 =$

15. $3.731 \times 444.7 =$

16. $51.4 \times .132 =$

Total Problems __16__ Problems Correct ____

Name_____     Skill:  Dividing Decimals

Divide.

1.  $8\overline{)3.2}$    2.  $6\overline{)6.0}$    3.  $3\overline{)3.6}$    4.  $6\overline{).24}$    5.  $7\overline{)3.5}$

6.  $3\overline{)2.7}$    7.  $8\overline{).88}$    8.  $4\overline{).36}$    9.  $4\overline{).12}$    10.  $9\overline{)4.5}$

11.  $5\overline{).30}$    12.  $8\overline{).48}$    13.  $.02\overline{)56}$    14.  $.7\overline{)84}$    15.  $.03\overline{)42}$

16.  $.6\overline{)54}$    17.  $.08\overline{)5.6}$    18.  $.5\overline{)6.0}$    19.  $.2\overline{).18}$    20.  $.4\overline{)2.8}$

Total Problems  20  Problems Correct ____

Name_____ Skill: Dividing Decimals

Divide. Round answers to the thousandths.

1.  $5\overline{)6.0}$

2.  $.12\overline{)36}$

3.  $.3\overline{)15}$

4.  $.04\overline{)1.20}$

5.  $.3\overline{)3.15}$

6.  $2.2\overline{)7.04}$

7.  $3\overline{).360}$

8.  $4.4\overline{)27.72}$

9.  $15\overline{)30.60}$

10.  $1.5\overline{)1.50}$

11.  $.20\overline{)700}$

12.  $.5\overline{)15.55}$

13.  $1.9\overline{)38.38}$

14.  $.06\overline{).306}$

15.  $5.2\overline{)18.72}$

16.  $6.6\overline{)15.18}$

Total Problems __16__  Problems Correct ____

Name_____

Divide.

1. $3\overline{\smash{)}4.8}$

2. $.12\overline{\smash{)}60}$

3. $.4\overline{\smash{)}16}$

4. $.06\overline{\smash{)}2.40}$

5. $.4\overline{\smash{)}4.56}$

6. $1.2\overline{\smash{)}2.40}$

7. $2\overline{\smash{)}.328}$

8. $2.3\overline{\smash{)}20.7}$

9. $15\overline{\smash{)}30.15}$

10. $1.5\overline{\smash{)}.975}$

11. $.20\overline{\smash{)}400}$

12. $.5\overline{\smash{)}25.05}$

13. $1.8\overline{\smash{)}10.8}$

14. $.05\overline{\smash{)}.725}$

15. $2.1\overline{\smash{)}20.16}$

16. $6.6\overline{\smash{)}66.66}$

Total Problems __16__ Problems Correct ____

Name_____ Skill: Changing Percentages to Decimals

Change the following percentages to decimals.

1. **30% =**        2. **45% =**        3. **60% =**        4. **80% =**

5. **33% =**        6. **20% =**        7. **12% =**        8. **5% =**

9. **13% =**        10. **90% =**        11. **27% =**        12. **110% =**

13. **34% =**        14. **115% =**        15. **45% =**        16. **155% =**

┌─────────────────────────────────────────────┐
│ **Total Problems  16   Problems Correct ____** │
└─────────────────────────────────────────────┘

Name_____

Change the following fractions and mixed numbers to percentages.

1. $\dfrac{1}{4}$ =

2. $\dfrac{2}{5}$ =

3. $\dfrac{49}{50}$ =

4. $\dfrac{17}{10}$ =

5. $\dfrac{1}{5}$ =

6. $\dfrac{7}{50}$ =

7. $\dfrac{2}{10}$ =

8. $\dfrac{31}{50}$ =

9. $\dfrac{13}{50}$ =

10. $\dfrac{9}{10}$ =

11. $\dfrac{3}{5}$ =

12. $\dfrac{3}{4}$ =

13. $\dfrac{7}{20}$ =

14. $\dfrac{7}{25}$ =

15. $\dfrac{3}{10}$ =

16. $1\dfrac{2}{5}$ =

17. $3\dfrac{31}{50}$ =

18. $1\dfrac{43}{50}$ =

19. $4\dfrac{4}{25}$ =

20. $4\dfrac{4}{8}$ =

21. $5\dfrac{1}{5}$ =

22. $4\dfrac{1}{4}$ =

23. $2\dfrac{8}{32}$ =

**Total Problems  23   Problems Correct ____**

Name_____     Skill: Changing Decimals to Percentages

Change the following decimals to percentages.

1. .3 =

2. .03 =

3. 4.03 =

4. 8.75 =

5. 87.5 =

6. .34 =

7. 1.67 =

8. 15.8 =

9. .04 =

10. 1.25 =

11. .16 =

12. 1.62 =

13. .8 =

14. 2.5 =

15. .375 =

16. .07 =

**Total Problems  16  Problems Correct ____**

Name_____    Skill: Changing Decimals to Percentages

Change the following decimals to percentages.

1. .59 =              2. 2.1 =              3. 63.4 =              4. .4 =

5. 2.3 =              6. .2 =               7. 5.4 =               8. .07 =

9. .52 =             10. .02 =             11. 3.34 =             12. .061 =

13. .375 =           14. .004 =           15. 2.217 =           16. .0342 =

Total Problems __16__ Problems Correct ____

44

Name_____

Solve. Write your answers in simplest form.

1. **17% of 200 = _____**          2. **25% of 90 = _____**

3. **35% of 50 = _____**          4. **15% of 150 = _____**

5. **85% of 60 = _____**          6. **65% of 80 = _____**

7. **10% of 50 = _____**          8. **100% of 8 = _____**

9. **32% of 40 = _____**          10. **25% of 30 = _____**

11. **75% of 40 = _____**          12. **10% of 96 = _____**

13. **60% of 80 = _____**          14. **12% of 80 = _____**

---

**Total Problems __14__ Problems Correct ____**

Solve. Write your answers in simplest form.

1. **8% of 180 =** _____

2. **32% of 15 =** _____

3. **80% of 540 =** _____

4. **25% of 132 =** _____

5. **25% of 40 =** _____

6. **1% of 70 =** _____

7. **4% of 180 =** _____

8. **120% of 90 =** _____

9. **33% of 69 =** _____

10. **62% of 48 =** _____

11. **120% of 80 =** _____

12. **30% of 70 =** _____

13. **40% of 20 =** _____

14. **30% of 140 =** _____

**Total Problems __14__  Problems Correct ____**

Name_____ Skill: Finding Percentages

Solve.

1. 10 is _____% of 100

2. 42 is _____% of 50

3. 40 is _____% of 20

4. 65 is _____% of 90

5. 75 is _____% of 70

6. 30 is _____% of 75

7. .8 is _____% of 80

8. 5 is _____% of 60

9. 20 is _____% of 100

10. 25 is _____% of 125

11. 15 is _____% of 60

12. 2 is _____% of .8

13. 50 is _____% of 33

14. 360 is _____% of 240

**Total Problems  14  Problems Correct ____**

Name_____

Solve.

1.  **9 is _____% of 18**

2.  **225 is _____% of 90**

3.  **120 is _____% of 160**

4.  **16 is _____% of 80**

5.  **7 is _____% of 5**

6.  **12 is _____% of 16**

7.  **4 is _____% of 40**

8.  **36 is _____% of 400**

9.  **30 is _____% of 120**

10. **45 is _____% of 60**

11. **16 is _____% of 40**

12. **78 is _____% of 104**

13. **42 is _____% of 56**

14. **30 is _____% of 50**

**Total Problems __14__ Problems Correct ____**

Name_____

Solve.

1. **18 is 75% of _____**

2. **5 is 10% of _____**

3. **4 is 25% of _____**

4. **70 is 175% of _____**

5. **9 is 100% of _____**

6. **60 is 150% of _____**

7. **.7 is 50% of _____**

8. **8 is 4% of _____**

9. **1 is 25% of _____**

10. **32 is 50% of _____**

11. **15 is 50% of _____**

12. **30 is 10% of _____**

13. **42 is 40% of _____**

14. **60 is 200% of _____**

**Total Problems __14__ Problems Correct ____**

Name_____

Solve.

1. **57 is 150% of** _____

2. **39 is 52% of** _____

3. **88 is 110% of** _____

4. **73 is 20% of** _____

5. **19 is 25% of** _____

6. **60 is 150% of** _____

7. **408 is 85% of** _____

8. **18 is 25% of** _____

9. **72 is 80% of** _____

10. **9 is 30% of** _____

11. **26 is 52% of** _____

12. **50 is 40% of** _____

13. **20 is 50% of** _____

14. **32 is 80% of** _____

**Total Problems __14__ Problems Correct ____**

Name_____

Solve.

1. $(20 - 5) \div 3 =$

2. $12 + (2 + 1) =$

3. $36 \div (3 \times 3) =$

4. $6 \div 2 \times 3 =$

5. $125 \div (37 - 12) =$

6. $(10 + 10) \div 2 =$

7. $(3 \times 8) \div 8 =$

8. $(42 - 35) \times 6 =$

9. $(6 \times 3) \div 9 =$

10. $(2 + 10) \times (8 - 4) =$

11. $(4 \times 6) \div 12 =$

12. $30 + (15 \div 5) =$

13. $(7 + 5) \times 4 =$

14. $(2 \times 3 + 12) \div 3 =$

**Total Problems  14   Problems Correct ____**

Solve.

1. $3 \times 3 \times 5 =$

2. $(6 + 4) \div 5 =$

3. $(25 \times 6) + 17 =$

4. $9 \div (6 - 3) =$

5. $(92 - 11) \div 9 =$

6. $(6 + 4) \times (14 - 2) =$

7. $144 \div 12 - 8 =$

8. $6 + 2 \times 15 =$

9. $(48 \div 6) \times 10 =$

10. $2 + 16 - 5 =$

11. $4 \times 6 + 8 - 15 =$

12. $(17 - 2) \div 3 =$

13. $(3 + 5) \div 2 + 4 - 6 =$

14. $(6 + 6) \div 2 - 4 - 1 =$

Total Problems 14  Problems Correct ____

Name_____

Solve.

1. **363 ÷ (7 − 4) =**

2. **64 ÷ (20 − 16) =**

3. **(6 + 5) x 2 + 3 =**

4. **12 x (8 + 4)**

5. **(6 + 2) x 4 =**

6. **2 x (4 + 10) =**

7. **8 − 6 + 12 =**

8. **25 x 3 + 78 =**

9. **(24 ÷ 6) x 11 =**

10. **3 + 18 − 5 =**

11. **(2 + 12) ÷ 7 =**

12. **4 x (17 + 20) =**

13. **(42 − 18) ÷ (10 − 4) =**

14. **(3 + 6) ÷ 3 − 1 − 1 =**

**Total Problems  14   Problems Correct ____**

Name_____

Solve.

1. $3 \times (16 + 27) =$

2. $(2 \times 16) \div 8 =$

3. $95 - 6 + 27 =$

4. $90 \div (50 - 40) =$

5. $32 \div 8 + 8 =$

6. $32 \div (8 + 8) =$

7. $(7 \times 6) \div 2 =$

8. $14 + (1 \times 7) =$

9. $(20 \div 5) \times 10 =$

10. $4 + 19 - 5 =$

11. $(3 + 18) \div 7 =$

12. $4 \times (16 + 20) =$

13. $(40 - 10) \div (10 - 5) =$

14. $(4 + 8) \div 3 - 2 - 0 =$

**Total Problems __14__  Problems Correct ____**

Name_____  Skill: Adding Integers

Add.

1.
$2 + {}^-7 =$

2.
${}^-7 + {}^-2 =$

3.
${}^-6 + 4 =$

4.
$9 + {}^-7 =$

5.
${}^-4 + 3 =$

6.
${}^-3 + {}^-6 =$

7.
${}^-1 + {}^-8 =$

8.
$5 + {}^-6 =$

9.
$9 + {}^-8 =$

10.
$11 + {}^-5 =$

11.
$2 + {}^-4 =$

12.
$4 + {}^-1 =$

13.
${}^-12 + {}^-3 =$

14.
${}^-8 + {}^-7 =$

15.
${}^-3 + {}^-4 =$

16.
$8 + {}^-2 =$

17.
$13 + {}^-1 =$

18.
$3 + {}^-4 =$

**Total Problems __18__  Problems Correct ____**

Name_____        Skill: Adding Integers

Add.

1. $42 + {}^-18 =$

2. ${}^-54 + {}^-87 =$

3. ${}^-61 + 40 =$

4. $90 + {}^-71 =$

5. ${}^-42 + 31 =$

6. ${}^-34 + {}^-62 =$

7. ${}^-12 + {}^-80 =$

8. $15 + {}^-61 =$

9. $3 + {}^-42 =$

10. $9 + {}^-4 =$

11. $22 + {}^-41 =$

12. $54 + {}^-1 =$

13. ${}^-18 + {}^-3 =$

14. ${}^-80 + {}^-79 =$

15. ${}^-5 + {}^-6 =$

16. $7 + {}^-3 =$

17. $14 + {}^-5 =$

18. $6 + {}^-8 =$

**Total Problems _18_ Problems Correct ____**

Add.

1.  $45 + {}^-78 =$

2.  ${}^-27 + {}^-2 =$

3.  ${}^-46 + 4 =$

4.  $15 + {}^-72 =$

5.  ${}^-40 + 35 =$

6.  ${}^-31 + {}^-61 =$

7.  ${}^-19 + {}^-82 =$

8.  $65 + {}^-6 =$

9.  $48 + {}^-82 =$

10. $65 + {}^-56 =$

11. $42 + {}^-48 =$

12. $18 + {}^-18 =$

13. ${}^-18 + {}^-32 =$

14. ${}^-17 + {}^-21 =$

15. ${}^-32 + {}^-42 =$

16. $25 + {}^-25 =$

17. $46 + {}^-18 =$

18. $25 + {}^-4 =$

**Total Problems  18   Problems Correct _____**

Name_____     Skill: Adding Integers

Add.

1. $^-26 + ^-16 =$

2. $^-32 + ^-15 =$

3. $^-20 + ^-30 =$

4. $27 + ^-18 =$

5. $^-41 + 23 =$

6. $^-33 + ^-66 =$

7. $^-17 + ^-82 =$

8. $^-55 + ^-66 =$

9. $91 + ^-81 =$

10. $14 + ^-3 =$

11. $77 + ^-82 =$

12. $44 + ^-14 =$

13. $^-62 + ^-27 =$

14. $^-51 + ^-38 =$

15. $^-23 + ^-24 =$

16. $88 + ^-35 =$

17. $21 + ^-19 =$

18. $33 + ^-40 =$

**Total Problems  18   Problems Correct ____**

Subtract.

1.
$$^-2 - 7 =$$

2.
$$5 - ^-7 =$$

3.
$$^-6 - ^-10 =$$

4.
$$4 - ^-1 =$$

5.
$$4 - ^-6 =$$

6.
$$^-8 - ^-3 =$$

7.
$$^-8 - ^-9 =$$

8.
$$^-3 - ^-7 =$$

9.
$$9 - ^-8 =$$

10.
$$5 - ^-2 =$$

11.
$$4 - ^-2 =$$

12.
$$5 - ^-3 =$$

13.
$$^-8 - ^-4 =$$

14.
$$^-9 - ^-3 =$$

15.
$$^-7 - ^-9 =$$

16.
$$8 - ^-4 =$$

17.
$$13 - ^-2 =$$

18.
$$2 - ^-3 =$$

**Total Problems __18__  Problems Correct ____**

Name_____

Skill: Subtracting Integers

Subtract.

1. $^-4 - 5 =$

2. $^-11 - ^-3 =$

3. $^-6 - ^-2 =$

4. $10 - 2 =$

5. $2 - ^-3 =$

6. $^-6 - ^-5 =$

7. $^-3 - ^-8 =$

8. $^-4 - ^-6 =$

9. $7 - ^-8 =$

10. $4 - ^-1 =$

11. $5 - ^-6 =$

12. $8 - ^-2 =$

13. $^-9 - ^-3 =$

14. $^-8 - ^-6 =$

15. $^-5 - ^-3 =$

16. $7 - ^-2 =$

17. $10 - ^-5 =$

18. $8 - ^-3 =$

**Total Problems _18_ Problems Correct ____**

© Carson-Dellosa CD-3750

60

Name_____   Skill: Subtracting Integers

Subtract.

1. $^-27 - 14 =$

2. $^-22 - ^-32 =$

3. $^-26 - ^-41 =$

4. $50 - 30 =$

5. $17 - ^-16 =$

6. $^-18 - ^-24 =$

7. $^-23 - ^-42 =$

8. $^-21 - ^-35 =$

9. $17 - ^-20 =$

10. $35 - ^-16 =$

11. $25 - ^-25 =$

12. $39 - ^-42 =$

13. $^-85 - ^-75 =$

14. $^-46 - ^-27 =$

15. $^-88 - ^-92 =$

16. $39 - ^-62 =$

17. $47 - ^-64 =$

18. $47 - ^-53 =$

Total Problems __18__ Problems Correct ____

Subtract.

1.  $^-42 - 34 =$

2.  $^-56 - ^-77 =$

3.  $^-50 - ^-62 =$

4.  $30 - ^-20 =$

5.  $^-48 - ^-52 =$

6.  $^-78 - ^-34 =$

7.  $^-83 - ^-62 =$

8.  $^-24 - ^-55 =$

9.  $37 - ^-50 =$

10.  $52 - ^-38 =$

11.  $45 - ^-37 =$

12.  $29 - ^-33 =$

13.  $^-70 - ^-70 =$

14.  $^-26 - ^-28 =$

15.  $^-68 - ^-90 =$

16.  $69 - ^-42 =$

17.  $37 - ^-60 =$

18.  $57 - ^-52 =$

**Total Problems  18  Problems Correct ____**

Name_____   Skill: Adding and Subtracting Integers

Solve.

1.
$^-42 - 34 + 15 =$

2.
$^-22 - ^-77 + 12 =$

3.
$1 + 15 - ^-4 =$

4.
$30 - ^-15 + ^-14 =$

5.
$^-8 - ^-4 + 5 =$

6.
$^-13 - ^-50 + 16 =$

7.
$36 - ^-21 - 12 =$

8.
$^-36 - ^-37 + 23 =$

9.
$^-40 + ^-60 - 13 =$

10.
$^-51 - ^-47 + ^-5 =$

11.
$^-14 + ^-10 + 4 =$

12.
$21 - ^-35 + 66 =$

Total Problems __12__ Problems Correct ____

63

Name_____     Skill: Adding and Subtracting Integers

Solve.

1. ⁻2 – 2 + 2 =

2. ⁻13 – ⁻14 + 10 =

3. 36 + 14 – ⁻31 =

4. 21 – ⁻26 + ⁻44 =

5. ⁻24 – ⁻31 + 19 =

6. ⁻16 – ⁻42 + 31 =

7. 21 – ⁻18 – 25 =

8. ⁻56 – ⁻45 + 3 =

9. ⁻21 + ⁻50 – 43 =

10. ⁻13 – ⁻12 + ⁻10 =

11. ⁻16 + ⁻12 + 5 =

12. 17 – ⁻22 + 18 =

**Total Problems 12 Problems Correct ____**

64

Name_____ 

Skill: Multiplying Integers

Multiply.

1. ⁻3 x 2 =

2. ⁻6 x 3 =

3. ⁻5 x ⁻7 =

4. 9 x ⁻3 =

5. ⁻6 x ⁻4 =

6. 2 x ⁻10 =

7. ⁻3 x 8 =

8. ⁻3 x 7 =

9. ⁻6 x ⁻2 =

10. 21 x ⁻25 =

11. ⁻10 x ⁻3 =

12. ⁻2 x 9 =

13. ⁻5 x 3 =

14. ⁻9 x ⁻6 =

15. ⁻7 x 3 =

16. ⁻16 x 2 =

17. 2 x ⁻18 =

18. 6 x ⁻2 =

**Total Problems  18   Problems Correct _____**

Name_____

Multiply.

1. ⁻5 x 11 =

2. ⁻7 x 2 =

3. ⁻8 x ⁻4 =

4. 6 x ⁻5 =

5. ⁻8 x ⁻2 =

6. 3 x ⁻12 =

7. ⁻5 x 9 =

8. ⁻4 x 8 =

9. ⁻7 x ⁻9 =

10. 18 x ⁻4 =

11. ⁻12 x ⁻2 =

12. ⁻4 x 7 =

13. ⁻6 x 8 =

14. ⁻4 x ⁻6 =

15. ⁻3 x 3 =

16. ⁻6 x 2 =

17. 2 x ⁻5 =

18. 0 x ⁻2 =

**Total Problems _18_ Problems Correct ____**

Name_____

Multiply.

1.
$^-42 \times 20 =$

2.
$^-18 \times 12 =$

3.
$^-23 \times ^-62 =$

4.
$21 \times ^-4 =$

5.
$^-33 \times ^-11 =$

6.
$9 \times ^-15 =$

7.
$^-16 \times 15 =$

8.
$^-12 \times 13 =$

9.
$^-20 \times ^-100 =$

10.
$16 \times ^-10 =$

11.
$^-15 \times ^-30 =$

12.
$^-2 \times 17 =$

13.
$^-9 \times 18 =$

14.
$^-22 \times ^-16 =$

15.
$^-18 \times 4 =$

16.
$^-30 \times 14 =$

17.
$12 \times ^-5 =$

18.
$30 \times ^-6 =$

**Total Problems __18__  Problems Correct ____**

Name_____     Skill: Multiplying Integers

Multiply.

1. $^-20 \times 10 =$

2. $^-15 \times 17 =$

3. $^-43 \times {}^-60 =$

4. $14 \times {}^-2 =$

5. $^-35 \times {}^-15 =$

6. $5 \times {}^-16 =$

7. $^-17 \times 2 =$

8. $^-9 \times 23 =$

9. $^-21 \times {}^-12 =$

10. $15 \times {}^-8 =$

11. $^-6 \times {}^-21 =$

12. $^-20 \times 27 =$

13. $^-5 \times 28 =$

14. $^-13 \times {}^-12 =$

15. $^-15 \times 2 =$

16. $^-11 \times 16 =$

17. $10 \times {}^-3 =$

18. $21 \times {}^-6 =$

**Total Problems _18_ Problems Correct ____**

Name_____ Skill: Multiplying Integers

Multiply.

1. ⁻5 x 15 =

2. ⁻21 x 32 =

3. ⁻18 x ⁻27 =

4. 21 x ⁻16 =

5. ⁻30 x ⁻22 =

6. 3 x ⁻90 =

7. ⁻10 x 3 =

8. ⁻8 x 11 =

9. ⁻15 x ⁻17 =

10. 12 x ⁻7 =

11. ⁻4 x ⁻22 =

12. ⁻21 x 30 =

13. ⁻8 x 22 =

14. ⁻15 x ⁻14 =

15. ⁻13 x 3 =

16. ⁻10 x 14 =

17. 12 x ⁻6 =

18. 31 x ⁻24 =

**Total Problems __18__ Problems Correct ____**

Name_____

Complete the following.

1. If t = 3, then 12 + t = _____

2. If u = 5, then 25 ÷ u = _____

3. If w = 4, then 10 – w = _____

4. If z = 5, then 11 x z = _____

5. If e = 9, then 6 + e = _____

6. If g = 2, then 4 ÷ g = _____

7. If q = 1, then q + 7 = _____

8. If s = 4, then 12 – s = _____

9. If k = 14, then 2 x k = _____

Total Problems _9_ Problems Correct ____

Complete the following.

1.  **If r = 6, then 10 + r = _____**

2.  **If c = 3, then 24 ÷ c = _____**

3.  **If x = 7, then 7 − x = _____**

4.  **If a = 4, then 10 x a = _____**

5.  **If f = 8, then 21 + f = _____**

6.  **If g = 3, then 9 ÷ g = _____**

7.  **If q = 8, then q + 9 = _____**

8.  **If m = 3, then 10 − m = _____**

9.  **If p = 16, then 1 x p = _____**

**Total Problems _9_  Problems Correct ____**

Name_____

Complete the following.

1. **If r = 2, then 15 + r = _____**

2. **If c = 12, then 36 ÷ c = _____**

3. **If x = 15, then 28 – x = _____**

4. **If a = 19, then 2 x a = _____**

5. **If f = 12, then 20 + f = _____**

6. **If g = 9, then 81 ÷ g = _____**

7. **If q = 16, then 23 + q = _____**

8. **If m = 21, then 35 – m = _____**

9. **If p = 18, then 3 x p = _____**

**Total Problems _9_ Problems Correct _____**

Name_____

Complete the following.

1.  **If r = 5, then 15 + r = _____**

2.  **If h = 15, then 45 ÷ h = _____**

3.  **If e = 31, then 88 – e = _____**

4.  **If n = 14, then 9 + n = _____**

5.  **If k = 41, then 15 + k = _____**

6.  **If p = 4, then 16 ÷ p = _____**

7.  **If w = 12, then 24 + w = _____**

8.  **If v = 35, then 36 – v = _____**

9.  **If s = 7, then 4 x s = _____**

**Total Problems _9_ Problems Correct ____**

Complete the following.

1. **If w = 5, then 18 + w = _____**

2. **If u = 13, then 39 ÷ u = _____**

3. **If e = 77, then 95 – e = _____**

4. **If y = 9, then 8 + y = _____**

5. **If r = 12, then 0 + r = _____**

6. **If t = 2, then 32 ÷ t = _____**

7. **If z = 15, then 21 + z = _____**

8. **If c = 16, then 42 – c = _____**

9. **If g = 9, then 5 x g = _____**

**Total Problems _9_ Problems Correct ____**

Skill:  Substituting the Value of One
or Two Variables

Solve using the following values: **a = 2, b = 3, c = 4, d = 5**

1. $a + 4 =$

2. $3c =$

3. $c + 15 =$

4. $b \times d =$

5. $d - a =$

6. $b + a =$

7. $3b =$

8. $a + 20 =$

9. $4c =$

10. $5 - a =$

11. $8 + c =$

12. $b + d =$

13. $a \times b =$

14. $2d =$

15. $15 + a =$

16. $30 + b =$

17. $c + b =$

18. $b \times c =$

**Total Problems  18  Problems Correct ____**

Skill:  Substituting the Value of One
or Two Variables

Solve using the following values: **a = 2, b = 5, c = 10**

1.   **2c =**

2.   **b + 4 =**

3.   **a + b =**

4.   **c + 10 =**

5.   **8 − b =**

6.   **b + b =**

7.   **3b =**

8.   **b + 20 =**

9.   **4c =**

10.   **30 − c =**

11.   **6b =**

12.   **bc =**

13.   **c − a =**

14.   **9c =**

15.   **15 + a =**

16.   **4 + a =**

17.   **c + 12 =**

18.   **3b =**

**Total Problems  18   Problems Correct ____**

Name_____

Skill: Substituting the Value of One or Two Variables

Solve using the following values: **f = 6, g = 8, i = 10, j = 12**

1. $j \div f =$

2. $j \times j =$

3. $2f =$

4. $22 - f =$

5. $16i =$

6. $16 + g =$

7. $24 - g =$

8. $f \times i =$

9. $4f =$

10. $g \times i =$

11. $10j =$

12. $g \times j =$

13. $100 \div i =$

14. $18 - j =$

15. $7 + f =$

16. $j - 6 =$

17. $j - f =$

18. $24 \div f =$

**Total Problems  18  Problems Correct ____**

77

Name_____

Skill: Substituting the Value of One or Two Variables

Solve using the following values: **k = 4, m = 6, n = 8, p = 10**

1. $2k + 4m =$

2. $4n \times p =$

3. $2p =$

4. $10n - p =$

5. $km \div 12 =$

6. $k + m =$

7. $np - 4 =$

8. $2m + p =$

9. $p - k =$

10. $4p - 2n =$

11. $8n + m =$

12. $pk =$

13. $np + 10 =$

14. $87 - np =$

15. $2p + 2n =$

16. $n - 6 =$

17. $m - 1 =$

18. $3mp =$

Total Problems __18__ Problems Correct _____

78

Name_____          Skill: Substituting the Value of One
                                                     or Two Variables

Solve using the following values: r = 3, s = 4, t = 5, u = 6

1. 2r + s =                2. 4s x 10 =               3. 2u =

4. 5u − 20 =              5. 2u ÷ r =                6. st =

7. ru − 2t =              8. u + 2t =                9. 5r − s =

10. 3s x r =             11. u ÷ r =                12. 2u + 4r =

13. 6t + r =             14. 2r − 3 =               15. t + u =

16. s x 3r =             17. u − 1 =                18. 3tu =

Total Problems __18__  Problems Correct ____

79

Find the value of each variable.

1.  $5 + x = 8$

2.  $4 = y - 16$

3.  $x - 6 = 8$

4.  $14 = 8 + x$

5.  $22 = a + 6$

6.  $3 + x = 4$

7.  $a + 16 = 37$

8.  $25 - y = 5$

9.  $35 = 60 - y$

10.  $y - 4 = 25$

11.  $16 - n = 9$

12.  $b + 5 = 42$

13.  $7 + c = 14$

14.  $28 - d = 12$

15.  $14 + f = 22$

16.  $a - 10 = 6$

17.  $12 + e = 46$

18.  $x + 14 = 16$

**Total Problems  18   Problems Correct _____**

Find the value of each variable.

1. $25 + a = 37$

2. $10 = a + 5$

3. $x - 9 = 16$

4. $30 = 7 + x$

5. $45 = j + 17$

6. $3 + x = 15$

7. $a + 12 = 44$

8. $30 - y = 6$

9. $25 = 20 - y$

10. $y - 9 = 16$

11. $14 - n = 2$

12. $t + 18 = 56$

13. $7 + e = 19$

14. $39 - r = 11$

15. $89 + n = 100$

16. $w - 15 = 7$

17. $13 + p = 23$

18. $a + 19 = 22$

**Total Problems  18   Problems Correct ____**

Find the value of each variable.

1. $4 + x = 8$

2. $3 = y - 17$

3. $x + 6 = 10$

4. $27 = 9 \times k$

5. $23 = y + 9$

6. $5 + e = 50$

7. $a + 13 = 41$

8. $30 - h = 9$

9. $75 = 90 - z$

10. $y - 2 = 47$

11. $18 - v = 6$

12. $s + 4 = 15$

13. $8 + r = 22$

14. $31 - d = 10$

15. $12 \times f = 144$

16. $\dfrac{x}{4} = 5$

17. $\dfrac{20}{c} = 5$

18. $\dfrac{x}{3} = 9$

Total Problems __18__ Problems Correct ____

Name_____

Skill: Finding the Value of
One Variable

Find the value of each variable.

1. $4r = 20$

2. $15 = 5a$

3. $2a - 20 = 10$

4. $80 = 11 + m$

5. $42 = a + 7$

6. $52 + t = 98$

7. $w + 36 = 39$

8. $75 - q = 0$

9. $21 = 40 - h$

10. $a - 44 = 20$

11. $12 \times n = 72$

12. $w \times 5 = 60$

13. $50 - c = 2$

14. $38 - e = 12$

15. $15 \times w = 15$

16. $\dfrac{c}{9} = 4$

17. $\dfrac{33}{c} = 3$

18. $\dfrac{r}{6} = 3$

**Total Problems  18   Problems Correct ____**

83

Solve.

1.  $2^2 = $ ___ X ___ = ___

2.  $5^2 = $ ___ X ___ = ___

3.  $10^2 = $ ___ X ___ = ___

4.  $14^2 = $ ___ X ___ = ___

5.  $6^2 = $ ___ X ___ = ___

6.  $3^2 = $ ___ X ___ = ___

7.  $1^2 = $ ___ X ___ = ___

8.  $13^2 = $ ___ X ___ = ___

9.  $9^2 = $ ___ X ___ = ___

10. $12^2 = $ ___ X ___ = ___

11. $8^2 = $ ___ X ___ = ___

12. $4^2 = $ ___ X ___ = ___

13. $15^2 = $ ___ X ___ = ___

14. $7^2 = $ ___ X ___ = ___

15. $16^2 = $ ___ X ___ = ___

16. $17^2 = $ ___ X ___ = ___

Total Problems  16  Problems Correct ____

Solve.

1. $2^2 =$       2. $20^2 =$      3. $12^2 =$      4. $6^2 =$

5. $13^2 =$      6. $3^2 =$      7. $17^2 =$      8. $22^2 =$

9. $16^2 =$      10. $14^2 =$      11. $4^2 =$      12. $21^2 =$

13. $5^2 =$      14. $10^2 =$      15. $7^2 =$      16. $15^2 =$

**Total Problems  16  Problems Correct ____**

Name_____

Solve.

1. $15^2 =$

2. $7^2 =$

3. $6^2 =$

4. $3^2 =$

5. $17^2 =$

6. $1^2 =$

7. $12^2 =$

8. $18^2 =$

9. $4^2 =$

10. $50^2 =$

11. $30^2 =$

12. $13^2 =$

13. $40^2 =$

14. $5^2 =$

15. $11^2 =$

16. $9^2 =$

**Total Problems  16   Problems Correct ____**

Solve.

1. $\sqrt{25}$ = $\sqrt{\rule{1cm}{0.15mm} \ X \ \rule{1cm}{0.15mm}}$ = ___

2. $\sqrt{144}$ = $\sqrt{\rule{1cm}{0.15mm} \ X \ \rule{1cm}{0.15mm}}$ = ___

3. $\sqrt{4}$ = $\sqrt{\rule{1cm}{0.15mm} \ X \ \rule{1cm}{0.15mm}}$ = ___

4. $\sqrt{100}$ = $\sqrt{\rule{1cm}{0.15mm} \ X \ \rule{1cm}{0.15mm}}$ = ___

5. $\sqrt{36}$ = $\sqrt{\rule{1cm}{0.15mm} \ X \ \rule{1cm}{0.15mm}}$ = ___

6. $\sqrt{64}$ = $\sqrt{\rule{1cm}{0.15mm} \ X \ \rule{1cm}{0.15mm}}$ = ___

7. $\sqrt{256}$ = $\sqrt{\rule{1cm}{0.15mm} \ X \ \rule{1cm}{0.15mm}}$ = ___

8. $\sqrt{625}$ = $\sqrt{\rule{1cm}{0.15mm} \ X \ \rule{1cm}{0.15mm}}$ = ___

9. $\sqrt{16}$ = $\sqrt{\rule{1cm}{0.15mm} \ X \ \rule{1cm}{0.15mm}}$ = ___

10. $\sqrt{121}$ = $\sqrt{\rule{1cm}{0.15mm} \ X \ \rule{1cm}{0.15mm}}$ = ___

11. $\sqrt{49}$ = $\sqrt{\rule{1cm}{0.15mm} \ X \ \rule{1cm}{0.15mm}}$ = ___

12. $\sqrt{961}$ = $\sqrt{\rule{1cm}{0.15mm} \ X \ \rule{1cm}{0.15mm}}$ = ___

**Total Problems __12__   Problems Correct ____**

Name_____

Find the square roots.

1. $\sqrt{4}$ =

2. $\sqrt{36}$ =

3. $\sqrt{900}$ =

4. $\sqrt{49}$ =

5. $\sqrt{81}$ =

6. $\sqrt{1}$ =

7. $\sqrt{100}$ =

8. $\sqrt{9}$ =

9. $\sqrt{169}$ =

10. $\sqrt{121}$ =

11. $\sqrt{324}$ =

12. $\sqrt{289}$ =

13. $\sqrt{16}$ =

14. $\sqrt{196}$ =

15. $\sqrt{400}$ =

16. $\sqrt{144}$ =

17. $\sqrt{64}$ =

18. $\sqrt{256}$ =

19. $\sqrt{225}$ =

20. $\sqrt{25}$ =

Total Problems __20__  Problems Correct _____

Name_____     Skill:  Finding Square Roots

Find the square roots.

1. $\sqrt{784} =$      2. $\sqrt{196} =$      3. $\sqrt{144} =$      4. $\sqrt{900} =$

5. $\sqrt{121} =$      6. $\sqrt{625} =$      7. $\sqrt{225} =$      8. $\sqrt{64} =$

9. $\sqrt{100} =$      10. $\sqrt{256} =$      11. $\sqrt{441} =$      12. $\sqrt{400} =$

13. $\sqrt{484} =$      14. $\sqrt{49} =$      15. $\sqrt{529} =$      16. $\sqrt{36} =$

17. $\sqrt{81} =$      18. $\sqrt{25} =$      19. $\sqrt{289} =$      20. $\sqrt{16} =$

**Total Problems  20   Problems Correct ____**

Name_____      Skill: Finding Exponents

Solve.

1. $3^3 =$      2. $7^2 =$      3. $4^3 =$      4. $6^3 =$

5. $2^3 =$      6. $5^3 =$      7. $8^3 =$      8. $9^3 =$

9. $1^3 =$      10. $8^4 =$      11. $6^4 =$      12. $2^4 =$

13. $5^4 =$      14. $9^4 =$      15. $3^4 =$      16. $5^4 =$

**Total Problems __16__ Problems Correct ____**

Solve.

1. $5^3 =$          2. $2^2 =$          3. $1^3 =$          4. $3^3 =$

5. $4^3 =$          6. $8^3 =$          7. $6^3 =$          8. $7^3 =$

9. $10^3 =$         10. $9^4 =$         11. $1^4 =$         12. $5^4 =$

13. $3^4 =$         14. $8^5 =$         15. $5^4 =$         16. $2^4 =$

**Total Problems  16   Problems Correct ____**

Solve.

1. $7^3 =$  2. $4^2 =$  3. $5^3 =$  4. $3^3 =$

5. $1^3 =$  6. $9^3 =$  7. $8^3 =$  8. $7^4 =$

9. $2^3 =$  10. $8^4 =$  11. $5^4 =$  12. $3^2 =$

13. $6^5 =$  14. $3^6 =$  15. $2^5 =$  16. $7^5 =$

**Total Problems  16  Problems Correct _____**

Solve.

1.  $2^6 =$

2.  $8^7 =$

3.  $4^6 =$

4.  $9^6 =$

5.  $3^7 =$

6.  $4^7 =$

7.  $8^6 =$

8.  $5^6 =$

9.  $7^7 =$

10. $2^7 =$

11. $3^6 =$

12. $5^4 =$

13. $6^7 =$

14. $1^5 =$

15. $2^5 =$

16. $7^4 =$

Total Problems __16__ Problems Correct ____

Solve.

1.  $3^6 =$          2.  $4^5 =$          3.  $2^5 =$          4.  $6^6 =$

5.  $10^5 =$         6.  $6^5 =$          7.  $10^6 =$         8.  $1^4 =$

9.  $8^6 =$          10. $2^6 =$          11. $3^5 =$          12. $4^6 =$

13. $11^6 =$         14. $8^5 =$          15. $5^7 =$         16. $11^5 =$

Total Problems __16__  Problems Correct ____

**94**

Solve.

1. $2^7 =$          2. $4^7 =$          3. $3^6 =$          4. $7^7 =$

5. $5^7 =$          6. $6^6 =$          7. $9^6 =$          8. $6^7 =$

9. $5^6 =$          10. $4^6 =$          11. $2^6 =$          12. $9^7 =$

13. $12^7 =$          14. $7^6 =$          15. $3^7 =$          16. $4^5 =$

Total Problems __16__  Problems Correct ____

Name_____ 　　　　　Skill:  Finding Exponents

Complete the chart.

| Base number | Second Power | Third Power | Fourth Power | Fifth Power | Sixth Power |
|:---:|:---:|:---:|:---:|:---:|:---:|
| 1 | | | | | |
| 2 | | | | | |
| 3 | | | | | |
| 4 | | | | | |
| 5 | | | | | |
| 6 | | | | | |
| 7 | | | | | |
| 8 | | | | | |
| 9 | | | | | |
| 10 | | | | | |

**Total Problems __10__ Problems Correct ____**

# Answer Key

© Carson-Dellosa CD-3750

---

**Page 1**

Name_____    Skill: Multiplication

Multiply.

| | | | | |
|---|---|---|---|---|
| 1. 423<br>x 6<br>2,538 | 2. 872<br>x 9<br>7,848 | 3. 584<br>x 2<br>1,168 | 4. 675<br>x 5<br>3,375 | 5. 862<br>x 4<br>3,448 |
| 6. 905<br>x 8<br>7,240 | 7. 782<br>x 3<br>2,346 | 8. 652<br>x 4<br>2,608 | 9. 483<br>x 21<br>10,143 | 10. 985<br>x 52<br>51,220 |
| 11. 125<br>x 10<br>1,250 | 12. 863<br>x 49<br>42,287 | 13. 187<br>x 28<br>5,236 | 14. 229<br>x 15<br>3,435 | 15. 697<br>x 54<br>37,638 |
| 16. 754<br>x 13<br>9,802 | 17. 237<br>x 95<br>22,515 | 18. 863<br>x 42<br>36,246 | 19. 307<br>x 72<br>22,104 | 20. 428<br>x 19<br>8,132 |

Total Problems _20_ Problems Correct ____

© Carson-Dellosa CD-3750
1

---

**Page 2**

Name_____    Skill: Multiplication

Multiply.

| | | | | |
|---|---|---|---|---|
| 1. 835<br>x 52<br>43,420 | 2. 298<br>x 42<br>12,516 | 3. 785<br>x 54<br>42,390 | 4. 962<br>x 16<br>15,392 | 5. 741<br>x 28<br>20,748 |
| 6. 284<br>x 625<br>177,500 | 7. 103<br>x 294<br>30,282 | 8. 786<br>x 528<br>415,008 | 9. 642<br>x 310<br>199,020 | 10. 925<br>x 652<br>603,100 |
| 11. 107<br>x 643<br>68,801 | 12. 822<br>x 467<br>383,874 | 13. 483<br>x 425<br>205,275 | 14. 819<br>x 652<br>533,988 | 15. 407<br>x 300<br>122,100 |
| 16. 925<br>x 462<br>427,350 | 17. 117<br>x 563<br>65,871 | 18. 628<br>x 413<br>259,364 | 19. 217<br>x 648<br>140,616 | 20. 394<br>x 225<br>88,650 |

Total Problems _20_ Problems Correct ____

© Carson-Dellosa CD-3750
2

---

**Page 3**

Name_____    Skill: Multiplication

Multiply.

| | | | | |
|---|---|---|---|---|
| 1. 1,248<br>x 73<br>91,104 | 2. 9,071<br>x 51<br>462,621 | 3. 8,265<br>x 49<br>404,985 | 4. 3,542<br>x 28<br>99,176 | 5. 2,331<br>x 78<br>181,818 |
| 6. 4,918<br>x 56<br>275,408 | 7. 7,510<br>x 50<br>375,500 | 8. 8,162<br>x 35<br>285,670 | 9. 4,076<br>x 328<br>1,336,928 | 10. 9,651<br>x 525<br>5,066,775 |
| 11. 8,600<br>x 315<br>2,709,000 | 12. 2,542<br>x 647<br>1,644,674 | 13. 1,359<br>x 689<br>936,351 | 14. 4,077<br>x 178<br>725,706 | 15. 3,007<br>x 848<br>2,549,936 |
| 16. 5,215<br>x 781<br>4,072,915 | 17. 4,252<br>x 843<br>3,584,436 | 18. 6,594<br>x 122<br>804,468 | 19. 3,103<br>x 212<br>657,836 | 20. 4,255<br>x 382<br>1,625,410 |

Total Problems _20_ Problems Correct ____

© Carson-Dellosa CD-3750
3

---

**Page 4**

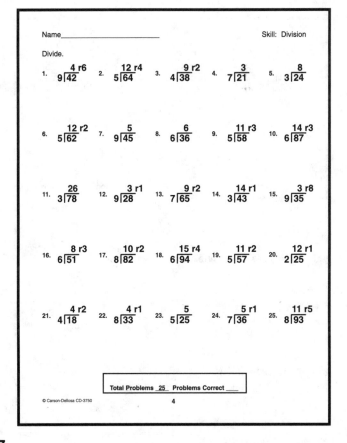

Name_____    Skill: Division

Divide.

| | | | | |
|---|---|---|---|---|
| 1. 4 r6<br>9)42 | 2. 12 r4<br>5)64 | 3. 9 r2<br>4)38 | 4. 3<br>7)21 | 5. 8<br>3)24 |
| 6. 12 r2<br>5)62 | 7. 5<br>9)45 | 8. 6<br>6)36 | 9. 11 r3<br>5)58 | 10. 14 r3<br>6)87 |
| 11. 26<br>3)78 | 12. 3 r1<br>9)28 | 13. 9 r2<br>7)65 | 14. 14 r1<br>3)43 | 15. 3 r8<br>9)35 |
| 16. 8 r3<br>6)51 | 17. 10 r2<br>8)82 | 18. 15 r4<br>6)94 | 19. 11 r2<br>5)57 | 20. 12 r1<br>2)25 |
| 21. 4 r2<br>4)18 | 22. 4 r1<br>8)33 | 23. 5<br>5)25 | 24. 5 r1<br>7)36 | 25. 11 r5<br>8)93 |

Total Problems _25_ Problems Correct ____

© Carson-Dellosa CD-3750
4

# Answer Key

## Panel 1 (page 5)

Divide.

1. $5\overline{)425} = 85$
2. $8\overline{)325} = 40\ r5$
3. $3\overline{)672} = 224$
4. $6\overline{)453} = 75\ r3$
5. $4\overline{)681} = 170\ r1$
6. $9\overline{)553} = 61\ r4$
7. $7\overline{)957} = 136\ r5$
8. $5\overline{)496} = 99\ r1$
9. $2\overline{)5,090} = 2545$
10. $38\overline{)7,231} = 190\ r11$
11. $32\overline{)4,852} = 151\ r20$
12. $26\overline{)2,569} = 98\ r21$
13. $3\overline{)1,542} = 514$
14. $2\overline{)5,128} = 2564$
15. $7\overline{)3,182} = 454\ r4$
16. $5\overline{)7,825} = 1565$
17. $4\overline{)9,760} = 2440$
18. $7\overline{)4,027} = 575\ r2$
19. $4\overline{)6,011} = 1502\ r3$
20. $6\overline{)8,304} = 1384$

Total Problems _20_  Problems Correct ___

© Carson-Dellosa CD-3750    5

## Panel 2 (page 6)

Divide.

1. $25\overline{)467} = 18\ r17$
2. $56\overline{)306} = 5\ r26$
3. $61\overline{)162} = 2\ r40$
4. $45\overline{)671} = 14\ r41$
5. $63\overline{)339} = 5\ r24$
6. $97\overline{)927} = 9\ r54$
7. $77\overline{)183} = 2\ r29$
8. $82\overline{)783} = 9\ r45$
9. $89\overline{)298} = 3\ r31$
10. $76\overline{)8,011} = 105\ r31$
11. $36\overline{)2,470} = 68\ r22$
12. $51\overline{)3,520} = 69\ r1$
13. $38\overline{)1,784} = 46\ r36$
14. $85\overline{)4,240} = 49\ r75$
15. $72\overline{)5,621} = 78\ r5$
16. $97\overline{)3,876} = 39\ r93$
17. $91\overline{)8,847} = 97\ r20$
18. $55\overline{)7,562} = 137\ r27$
19. $68\overline{)2,513} = 36\ r65$
20. $24\overline{)6,628} = 276\ r4$

Total Problems _20_  Problems Correct ___

© Carson-Dellosa CD-3750    6

## Panel 3 (page 7)

Divide.

1. $21\overline{)1,247} = 59\ r8$
2. $51\overline{)4,320} = 84\ r36$
3. $42\overline{)5,794} = 137\ r40$
4. $35\overline{)2,395} = 68\ r15$
5. $75\overline{)5,321} = 70\ r71$
6. $67\overline{)3,072} = 45\ r57$
7. $52\overline{)7,894} = 151\ r42$
8. $86\overline{)6,190} = 71\ r84$
9. $49\overline{)3,437} = 70\ r7$
10. $83\overline{)6,235} = 75\ r10$
11. $22\overline{)1,384} = 62\ r20$
12. $47\overline{)4,718} = 100\ r18$
13. $56\overline{)2,357} = 42\ r5$
14. $34\overline{)8,532} = 250\ r32$
15. $99\overline{)4,796} = 48\ r44$
16. $73\overline{)5,060} = 69\ r23$
17. $68\overline{)9,949} = 146\ r21$
18. $71\overline{)3,218} = 45\ r23$
19. $26\overline{)7,198} = 276\ r22$
20. $37\overline{)6,217} = 168\ r1$

Total Problems _20_  Problems Correct ___

© Carson-Dellosa CD-3750    7

## Panel 4 (page 8)

Change each fraction or mixed number to simplest form.

1. $\frac{20}{25} = \frac{4}{5}$
2. $\frac{50}{70} = \frac{5}{7}$
3. $\frac{25}{35} = \frac{5}{7}$
4. $\frac{32}{64} = \frac{1}{2}$
5. $\frac{10}{25} = \frac{2}{5}$
6. $\frac{7}{49} = \frac{1}{7}$
7. $\frac{35}{42} = \frac{5}{6}$
8. $\frac{12}{18} = \frac{2}{3}$
9. $\frac{19}{38} = \frac{1}{2}$
10. $\frac{56}{63} = \frac{8}{9}$
11. $\frac{32}{80} = \frac{2}{5}$
12. $\frac{49}{56} = \frac{7}{8}$
13. $\frac{27}{36} = \frac{3}{4}$
14. $\frac{12}{20} = \frac{3}{5}$
15. $\frac{30}{42} = \frac{5}{7}$
16. $2\frac{16}{36} = 2\frac{4}{9}$
17. $3\frac{25}{60} = 3\frac{5}{12}$
18. $1\frac{10}{20} = 1\frac{1}{2}$
19. $4\frac{4}{40} = 4\frac{1}{10}$
20. $4\frac{24}{30} = 4\frac{4}{5}$
21. $3\frac{10}{15} = 3\frac{2}{3}$
22. $3\frac{3}{9} = 3\frac{1}{3}$
23. $8\frac{8}{16} = 8\frac{1}{2}$

Total Problems _23_  Problems Correct ___

© Carson-Dellosa CD-3750    8

# Answer Key

---

Skill: Changing Fractions to Simplest Form

Change each fraction or mixed number to simplest form.

1. $\frac{25}{50} = \frac{1}{2}$    2. $\frac{35}{75} = \frac{7}{15}$    3. $\frac{15}{25} = \frac{3}{5}$    4. $\frac{16}{18} = \frac{8}{9}$    5. $\frac{32}{60} = \frac{8}{15}$

6. $\frac{5}{20} = \frac{1}{4}$    7. $\frac{9}{81} = \frac{1}{9}$    8. $\frac{50}{60} = \frac{5}{6}$    9. $\frac{55}{75} = \frac{11}{15}$    10. $\frac{42}{49} = \frac{6}{7}$

11. $\frac{12}{36} = \frac{1}{3}$    12. $\frac{48}{52} = \frac{12}{13}$    13. $\frac{93}{663} = \frac{31}{221}$    14. $\frac{45}{81} = \frac{5}{9}$    15. $\frac{21}{28} = \frac{3}{4}$

16. $6\frac{35}{70} = 6\frac{1}{2}$    17. $9\frac{45}{60} = 9\frac{3}{4}$    18. $4\frac{28}{56} = 4\frac{1}{2}$    19. $5\frac{2}{92} = 5\frac{1}{46}$

20. $3\frac{2}{8} = 3\frac{1}{4}$    21. $7\frac{24}{36} = 7\frac{2}{3}$    22. $8\frac{9}{9} = 9$    23. $5\frac{9}{27} = 5\frac{1}{3}$

| Total Problems _23_  Problems Correct ____ |
| --- |

9

---

Skill: Changing Improper Fractions to Mixed Numbers

Change each fraction to a mixed number.

1. $\frac{36}{24} = 1\frac{1}{2}$    2. $\frac{90}{36} = 2\frac{1}{2}$    3. $\frac{48}{42} = 1\frac{1}{7}$    4. $\frac{50}{15} = 3\frac{1}{3}$    5. $\frac{19}{12} = 1\frac{7}{12}$

6. $\frac{50}{41} = 1\frac{9}{41}$    7. $\frac{9}{6} = 1\frac{1}{2}$    8. $\frac{47}{16} = 2\frac{15}{16}$    9. $\frac{55}{13} = 4\frac{3}{13}$    10. $\frac{62}{27} = 2\frac{8}{27}$

11. $\frac{41}{33} = 1\frac{8}{33}$    12. $\frac{48}{36} = 1\frac{1}{3}$    13. $\frac{23}{13} = 1\frac{10}{13}$    14. $\frac{57}{28} = 2\frac{1}{28}$    15. $\frac{23}{18} = 1\frac{5}{18}$

16. $\frac{98}{45} = 2\frac{8}{45}$    17. $\frac{76}{36} = 2\frac{1}{9}$    18. $\frac{16}{13} = 1\frac{3}{13}$    19. $\frac{45}{21} = 2\frac{1}{7}$    20. $\frac{21}{15} = 1\frac{2}{5}$

21. $\frac{12}{11} = 1\frac{1}{11}$    22. $\frac{92}{52} = 1\frac{10}{13}$    23. $\frac{85}{36} = 2\frac{13}{36}$    24. $\frac{92}{81} = 1\frac{11}{81}$    25. $\frac{38}{37} = 1\frac{1}{37}$

| Total Problems _25_  Problems Correct ____ |
| --- |

10

---

Skill: Changing Mixed Numbers to Fractions

Change each mixed number to a fraction.

1. $1\frac{2}{5} = \frac{7}{5}$    2. $3\frac{5}{6} = \frac{23}{6}$    3. $9\frac{2}{7} = \frac{65}{7}$

4. $6\frac{1}{5} = \frac{31}{5}$    5. $6\frac{1}{4} = \frac{25}{4}$    6. $7\frac{1}{2} = \frac{15}{2}$

7. $2\frac{1}{8} = \frac{17}{8}$    8. $9\frac{2}{3} = \frac{29}{3}$    9. $1\frac{3}{5} = \frac{8}{5}$

10. $4\frac{1}{7} = \frac{29}{7}$    11. $4\frac{5}{8} = \frac{37}{8}$    12. $5\frac{3}{8} = \frac{43}{8}$

| Total Problems _12_  Problems Correct ____ |
| --- |

11

---

Skill: Multiplying Fractions

Multiply. Write answers in simplest form.

1. $\frac{1}{4} \times \frac{2}{5} = \frac{1}{10}$    2. $\frac{1}{2} \times \frac{7}{8} = \frac{7}{16}$    3. $\frac{3}{8} \times \frac{2}{9} = \frac{1}{12}$

4. $\frac{1}{5} \times \frac{5}{6} = \frac{1}{6}$    5. $\frac{3}{5} \times \frac{5}{8} = \frac{3}{8}$    6. $\frac{9}{10} \times \frac{3}{7} = \frac{27}{70}$

7. $\frac{2}{3} \times \frac{3}{4} = \frac{1}{2}$    8. $\frac{1}{7} \times \frac{3}{5} = \frac{3}{35}$    9. $\frac{5}{8} \times \frac{1}{6} = \frac{5}{48}$

10. $\frac{1}{3} \times \frac{1}{9} = \frac{1}{27}$    11. $\frac{2}{9} \times \frac{1}{8} = \frac{1}{36}$    12. $\frac{7}{8} \times \frac{1}{4} = \frac{7}{32}$

13. $\frac{3}{4} \times \frac{7}{8} = \frac{21}{32}$    14. $\frac{2}{3} \times \frac{5}{9} = \frac{10}{27}$    15. $\frac{1}{4} \times \frac{3}{4} = \frac{3}{16}$

| Total Problems _15_  Problems Correct ____ |
| --- |

12

---

# Answer Key

Name_____

Skill: Multiplying Fractions

Multiply. Write answers in simplest form.

1. $\frac{1}{7} \times \frac{1}{2} = \frac{1}{14}$   2. $\frac{3}{4} \times \frac{5}{7} = \frac{15}{28}$   3. $\frac{2}{9} \times \frac{3}{5} = \frac{2}{15}$

4. $\frac{2}{5} \times \frac{2}{5} = \frac{4}{25}$   5. $\frac{3}{8} \times \frac{1}{2} = \frac{3}{16}$   6. $\frac{4}{5} \times \frac{3}{6} = \frac{2}{5}$

7. $\frac{3}{5} \times \frac{1}{6} = \frac{1}{10}$   8. $\frac{5}{7} \times \frac{2}{9} = \frac{10}{63}$   9. $\frac{8}{9} \times \frac{6}{7} = \frac{16}{21}$

10. $\frac{2}{5} \times \frac{4}{7} = \frac{8}{35}$   11. $\frac{3}{6} \times \frac{7}{8} = \frac{7}{16}$   12. $\frac{5}{6} \times \frac{1}{3} = \frac{5}{18}$

13. $\frac{5}{9} \times \frac{4}{8} = \frac{5}{18}$   14. $\frac{3}{7} \times \frac{1}{5} = \frac{3}{35}$   15. $\frac{1}{3} \times \frac{1}{5} = \frac{1}{15}$

Total Problems 15  Problems Correct ___

© Carson-Dellosa CD-3750

13

---

Name_____

Skill: Multiplying Fractions and Whole Numbers

Multiply. Write answers in simplest form.

1. $9 \times 3\frac{1}{3} = 30$   2. $8 \times 1\frac{1}{8} = 9$   3. $6 \times 1\frac{4}{9} = 8\frac{2}{3}$

4. $3 \times 5\frac{1}{5} = 15\frac{3}{5}$   5. $6 \times 3\frac{1}{6} = 19$   6. $7 \times 2\frac{3}{5} = 18\frac{1}{5}$

7. $9 \times 4\frac{3}{5} = 41\frac{2}{5}$   8. $7 \times 2\frac{5}{6} = 19\frac{5}{6}$   9. $2 \times 1\frac{1}{2} = 3$

10. $1 \times 8\frac{1}{12} = 8\frac{1}{12}$   11. $4 \times 8\frac{1}{3} = 33\frac{1}{3}$   12. $6 \times 2\frac{1}{5} = 13\frac{1}{5}$

Total Problems 12  Problems Correct ___

© Carson-Dellosa CD-3750

14

---

Name_____

Skill: Multiplying Mixed Numbers

Multiply. Write answers in simplest form.

1. $3\frac{1}{3} \times 9\frac{1}{2} = 31\frac{2}{3}$   2. $8\frac{1}{6} \times 2\frac{3}{5} = 21\frac{7}{30}$   3. $9\frac{2}{7} \times 4\frac{1}{5} = 39$

4. $4\frac{1}{5} \times 5\frac{1}{2} = 23\frac{1}{10}$   5. $5\frac{2}{5} \times 4\frac{4}{9} = 24$   6. $5\frac{1}{8} \times 8\frac{1}{3} = 42\frac{17}{24}$

7. $1\frac{3}{7} \times 4\frac{3}{4} = 6\frac{11}{14}$   8. $2\frac{6}{7} \times 5\frac{1}{4} = 15$   9. $4\frac{5}{8} \times 8\frac{2}{7} = 38\frac{9}{28}$

10. $1\frac{3}{4} \times 8\frac{3}{4} = 15\frac{5}{16}$   11. $3\frac{2}{3} \times 1\frac{3}{8} = 5\frac{1}{24}$   12. $8\frac{4}{9} \times 2\frac{5}{6} = 23\frac{25}{27}$

Total Problems 12  Problems Correct ___

© Carson-Dellosa CD-3750

15

---

Name_____

Skill: Dividing Fractions

Divide. Write answers in simplest form.

1. $\frac{1}{2} \div \frac{3}{4} = \frac{2}{3}$   2. $\frac{5}{16} \div \frac{5}{8} = \frac{1}{2}$   3. $\frac{8}{9} \div \frac{14}{15} = \frac{20}{21}$

4. $\frac{3}{4} \div \frac{13}{16} = \frac{12}{13}$   5. $\frac{3}{4} \div \frac{1}{2} = 1\frac{1}{2}$   6. $\frac{3}{5} \div \frac{3}{12} = 2\frac{2}{5}$

7. $\frac{8}{15} \div \frac{4}{5} = \frac{2}{3}$   8. $\frac{4}{5} \div \frac{4}{7} = 1\frac{2}{5}$   9. $\frac{4}{10} \div \frac{15}{27} = \frac{18}{25}$

10. $\frac{3}{4} \div \frac{1}{8} = 6$   11. $\frac{5}{10} \div \frac{12}{25} = 1\frac{1}{24}$   12. $\frac{21}{40} \div \frac{7}{24} = 1\frac{4}{5}$

13. $\frac{25}{38} \div \frac{15}{32} = 1\frac{23}{57}$   14. $\frac{7}{8} \div \frac{1}{2} = 1\frac{3}{4}$   15. $\frac{7}{12} \div \frac{14}{28} = 1\frac{1}{6}$

Total Problems 15  Problems Correct ___

© Carson-Dellosa CD-3750

16

© Carson-Dellosa CD-3750

100

# Answer Key

---

Divide. Write answers in simplest form.

1. $\frac{7}{50} \div \frac{21}{35} = \frac{7}{30}$  2. $\frac{7}{12} \div \frac{5}{6} = \frac{7}{10}$  3. $\frac{3}{4} \div \frac{27}{36} = 1$

4. $\frac{1}{2} \div \frac{4}{9} = 1\frac{1}{8}$  5. $\frac{7}{10} \div \frac{1}{6} = 4\frac{1}{5}$  6. $\frac{7}{12} \div \frac{14}{15} = \frac{5}{8}$

7. $\frac{7}{12} \div \frac{1}{2} = 1\frac{1}{6}$  8. $\frac{2}{3} \div \frac{8}{9} = \frac{3}{4}$  9. $\frac{1}{10} \div \frac{15}{30} = \frac{1}{5}$

10. $\frac{1}{7} \div \frac{1}{3} = \frac{3}{7}$  11. $\frac{5}{10} \div \frac{12}{25} = 1\frac{1}{24}$  12. $\frac{18}{33} \div \frac{6}{11} = 1$

13. $\frac{25}{36} \div \frac{5}{27} = 3\frac{3}{4}$  14. $\frac{1}{6} \div \frac{1}{3} = \frac{1}{2}$  15. $\frac{7}{12} \div \frac{5}{6} = \frac{7}{10}$

Total Problems _15_ Problems Correct ____

17

---

Divide. Write answers in simplest form.

1. $2 \div 1\frac{1}{2} = 1\frac{1}{3}$  2. $9 \div 3\frac{1}{3} = 2\frac{7}{10}$  3. $2 \div 2\frac{1}{4} = \frac{8}{9}$

4. $6 \div 4\frac{5}{6} = 1\frac{7}{29}$  5. $7 \div 7\frac{3}{4} = \frac{28}{31}$  6. $6 \div 6\frac{1}{9} = \frac{54}{55}$

7. $5 \div 3\frac{2}{5} = 1\frac{8}{17}$  8. $11 \div 5\frac{7}{8} = 1\frac{41}{47}$  9. $9 \div 2\frac{5}{6} = 3\frac{3}{17}$

10. $4 \div 4\frac{4}{5} = \frac{5}{6}$  11. $2 \div 5\frac{3}{5} = \frac{5}{14}$  12. $3 \div 4\frac{1}{6} = \frac{18}{25}$

13. $6 \div 2\frac{1}{2} = 2\frac{2}{5}$  14. $4 \div 1\frac{1}{4} = 3\frac{1}{5}$  15. $8 \div 4\frac{1}{2} = 1\frac{7}{9}$

Total Problems _15_ Problems Correct ____

18

---

Divide. Write answers in simplest form.

1. $1\frac{1}{2} \div 2\frac{2}{3} = \frac{9}{16}$  2. $4\frac{2}{3} \div 1\frac{7}{9} = 2\frac{5}{8}$  3. $1\frac{5}{6} \div 2\frac{2}{3} = \frac{11}{16}$

4. $5\frac{1}{4} \div 1\frac{1}{8} = 4\frac{2}{3}$  5. $5\frac{1}{7} \div 5\frac{1}{3} = \frac{27}{28}$  6. $4\frac{2}{7} \div 5\frac{1}{4} = \frac{40}{49}$

7. $2\frac{1}{7} \div 8\frac{4}{7} = \frac{1}{4}$  8. $4\frac{2}{7} \div 1\frac{1}{5} = 3\frac{4}{7}$  9. $5\frac{3}{5} \div 2\frac{2}{5} = 2\frac{1}{3}$

10. $9\frac{1}{6} \div 8\frac{1}{4} = 1\frac{1}{9}$  11. $3\frac{1}{4} \div 1\frac{7}{8} = 1\frac{11}{15}$  12. $4\frac{4}{9} \div 6\frac{2}{3} = \frac{2}{3}$

Total Problems _12_ Problems Correct ____

19

---

List the factors for each pair of numbers and find the greatest common factor.

|    |        | Factors | Greatest Common Factor |
|----|--------|---------|------------------------|
| 1. | 27, 36 | 27= 1,3,9,27  36= 1,2,3,4,6,9,12,18,36 | 9 |
| 2. | 42, 49 | 42= 1,2,3,6,7,14,21,42  49= 1,7,49 | 7 |
| 3. | 15, 18 | 15= 1,3,5,15  18= 1,2,3,6,9,18 | 3 |
| 4. | 16, 24 | 16= 1,2,4,8,16  24= 1,2,3,4,6,8,12,24 | 8 |
| 5. | 20, 40 | 20= 1,2,4,5,10,20  40= 1,2,4,5,8,10,20,40 | 20 |
| 6. | 63, 81 | 63= 1,3,7,9,21,63  81= 1,3,9,27,81 | 9 |
| 7. | 25, 50 | 25= 1,5,25  50= 1,2,5,10,25,50 | 25 |
| 8. | 36, 48 | 36= 1,2,3,4,6,9,12,18,36  48= 1,2,3,4,6,8,12,16,24,48 | 12 |
| 9. | 44, 66 | 44= 1, 2, 4, 11, 22, 44  66= 1, 2,3,6,11,22,33,66 | 22 |
| 10. | 22, 33 | 22= 1,2,11,22  33= 1,3,11,33 | 11 |

Total Problems _10_ Problems Correct ____

20

---

# Answer Key

---

Name_____  Skill: Finding the Greatest Common Factor

Find the greatest common factor for each pair of numbers.

1. 72, 90 ___18___
2. 24, 32 ___8___
3. 15, 30 ___15___
4. 36, 27 ___9___
5. 52, 32 ___4___
6. 36, 81 ___9___
7. 50, 20 ___10___
8. 16, 20 ___4___
9. 24, 46 ___2___
10. 48, 56 ___8___
11. 42, 81, 51 ___3___
12. 18, 21, 9 ___3___
13. 24, 16, 32 ___8___
14. 49, 28, 21 ___7___

Total Problems _14_ Problems Correct ____

© Carson-Dellosa CD-3750

21

---

Name_____  Skill: Finding the Least Common Multiple

Find the least common multiple of each pair of numbers.

1. 3, 5 ___15___
2. 5, 10 ___10___
3. 4, 3 ___12___
4. 2, 10 ___10___
5. 8, 12 ___24___
6. 9, 12 ___36___
7. 7, 8 ___56___
8. 6, 9 ___18___
9. 7, 4 ___28___
10. 11, 10 ___110___
11. 15, 25 ___75___
12. 8, 3 ___24___
13. 5, 7 ___35___
14. 9, 3 ___9___

Total Problems _14_ Problems Correct ____

© Carson-Dellosa CD-3750

22

---

Name_____  Skill: Finding the Least Common Multiple

Find the least common multiple of each set of numbers.

1. 2, 4 ___4___
2. 8, 3 ___24___
3. 5, 3 ___15___
4. 6, 9 ___18___
5. 12, 24 ___24___
6. 20, 30 ___60___
7. 8, 4 ___8___
8. 12, 18 ___36___
9. 10, 15 ___30___
10. 6, 10 ___30___
11. 9, 8, 12 ___72___
12. 7, 9 ___63___
13. 2, 7, 14 ___14___
14. 15, 30 ___30___

Total Problems _14_ Problems Correct ____

© Carson-Dellosa CD-3750

23

---

Name_____  Skill: Adding Fractions

Add. Write answers in simplest form.

1. $\frac{1}{4} + \frac{3}{5} = \frac{17}{20}$
2. $\frac{1}{2} + \frac{2}{3} = 1\frac{1}{6}$
3. $\frac{7}{8} + \frac{5}{6} = 1\frac{17}{24}$
4. $\frac{3}{4} + \frac{2}{7} = 1\frac{1}{28}$
5. $\frac{2}{7} + \frac{5}{14} = \frac{9}{14}$
6. $\frac{7}{8} + \frac{1}{7} = 1\frac{1}{56}$
7. $\frac{7}{9} + \frac{3}{3} = 1\frac{7}{9}$
8. $\frac{1}{3} + \frac{3}{8} = \frac{17}{24}$
9. $\frac{5}{8} + \frac{1}{6} = \frac{19}{24}$
10. $\frac{1}{7} + \frac{2}{9} = \frac{23}{63}$
11. $\frac{2}{6} + \frac{1}{8} = \frac{11}{24}$
12. $\frac{3}{7} + \frac{1}{4} = \frac{19}{28}$
13. $\frac{5}{9} + \frac{7}{8} = 1\frac{31}{72}$
14. $\frac{1}{6} + \frac{5}{8} = \frac{19}{24}$
15. $\frac{5}{8} + \frac{3}{7} = 1\frac{3}{56}$

Total Problems _15_ Problems Correct ____

© Carson-Dellosa CD-3750

24

---

© Carson-Dellosa CD-3750

102

# Answer Key

---

Name_____

Skill: Adding Fractions

Add. Write answers in simplest form.

1. $\frac{1}{3} + \frac{2}{3} = 1$   2. $\frac{5}{6} + \frac{1}{3} = 1\frac{1}{6}$   3. $\frac{4}{5} + \frac{1}{3} = 1\frac{2}{15}$

4. $\frac{3}{5} + \frac{1}{4} = \frac{17}{20}$   5. $\frac{3}{8} + \frac{5}{16} = \frac{11}{16}$   6. $\frac{2}{5} + \frac{1}{2} = \frac{9}{10}$

7. $\frac{5}{6} + \frac{1}{3} = 1\frac{1}{6}$   8. $\frac{1}{2} + \frac{2}{7} = \frac{11}{14}$   9. $\frac{5}{6} + \frac{1}{5} = 1\frac{1}{30}$

10. $\frac{1}{6} + \frac{2}{3} = \frac{5}{6}$   11. $\frac{2}{7} + \frac{1}{2} = \frac{11}{14}$   12. $\frac{5}{6} + \frac{1}{3} = 1\frac{1}{6}$

13. $\frac{1}{6} + \frac{1}{8} = \frac{7}{24}$   14. $\frac{4}{9} + \frac{3}{8} = \frac{59}{72}$   15. $\frac{2}{3} + \frac{2}{5} = 1\frac{1}{15}$

Total Problems **15** Problems Correct _____

25

---

Name_____

Skill: Subtracting Fractions

Subtract. Write answers in simplest form.

1. $\frac{4}{5} - \frac{3}{5} = \frac{1}{5}$   2. $\frac{3}{6} - \frac{1}{6} = \frac{1}{3}$   3. $\frac{4}{5} - \frac{2}{5} = \frac{2}{5}$

4. $\frac{3}{5} - \frac{1}{5} = \frac{2}{5}$   5. $\frac{5}{16} - \frac{2}{16} = \frac{3}{16}$   6. $\frac{2}{8} - \frac{1}{8} = \frac{1}{8}$

7. $\frac{5}{6} - \frac{1}{6} = \frac{2}{3}$   8. $\frac{7}{9} - \frac{2}{9} = \frac{5}{9}$   9. $\frac{1}{8} - \frac{1}{8} = 0$

10. $\frac{3}{4} - \frac{2}{4} = \frac{1}{4}$   11. $\frac{5}{7} - \frac{1}{7} = \frac{4}{7}$   12. $\frac{2}{2} - \frac{1}{2} = \frac{1}{2}$

13. $\frac{1}{3} - \frac{1}{3} = 0$   14. $\frac{4}{9} - \frac{3}{9} = \frac{1}{9}$   15. $\frac{3}{5} - \frac{2}{5} = \frac{1}{5}$

Total Problems **15** Problems Correct _____

26

---

Name_____

Skill: Subtracting Fractions From Whole Numbers

Subtract. Write answers in simplest form.

1. $2 - \frac{7}{8} = 1\frac{1}{8}$   2. $4 - \frac{2}{5} = 3\frac{3}{5}$   3. $5 - \frac{2}{3} = 4\frac{1}{3}$   4. $6 - \frac{1}{8} = 5\frac{7}{8}$

5. $3 - \frac{3}{4} = 2\frac{1}{4}$   6. $8 - \frac{9}{10} = 7\frac{1}{10}$   7. $7 - \frac{4}{5} = 6\frac{1}{5}$   8. $4 - \frac{3}{10} = 3\frac{7}{10}$

9. $5 - \frac{6}{9} = 4\frac{1}{3}$   10. $4 - \frac{2}{6} = 3\frac{2}{3}$   11. $5 - \frac{2}{5} = 4\frac{3}{5}$   12. $10 - \frac{1}{2} = 9\frac{1}{2}$

13. $12 - \frac{5}{7} = 11\frac{2}{7}$   14. $9 - \frac{1}{3} = 8\frac{2}{3}$   15. $4 - \frac{7}{8} = 3\frac{1}{8}$   16. $3 - \frac{6}{7} = 2\frac{1}{7}$

Total Problems **16** Problems Correct _____

27

---

Name_____

Skill: Subtracting Fractions and Whole and Mixed Numbers

Subtract. Write answers in simplest form.

1. $15\frac{3}{8} - \frac{3}{8} = 15$   2. $10\frac{1}{2} - \frac{2}{5} = 10\frac{1}{10}$   3. $1 - \frac{1}{3} = \frac{2}{3}$   4. $2 - \frac{6}{11} = 1\frac{5}{11}$

5. $5 - \frac{3}{5} = 4\frac{2}{5}$   6. $9 - \frac{3}{7} = 8\frac{4}{7}$   7. $14 - \frac{2}{9} = 13\frac{7}{9}$   8. $13 - \frac{2}{3} = 12\frac{1}{3}$

9. $1 - \frac{7}{8} = \frac{1}{8}$   10. $6 - \frac{1}{5} = 5\frac{4}{5}$   11. $7 - \frac{5}{6} = 6\frac{1}{6}$   12. $5 - \frac{1}{4} = 4\frac{3}{4}$

13. $8 - \frac{3}{4} = 7\frac{1}{4}$   14. $4 - \frac{1}{2} = 3\frac{1}{2}$   15. $2\frac{1}{3} - \frac{1}{6} = 2\frac{1}{6}$   16. $6 - \frac{3}{7} = 5\frac{4}{7}$

Total Problems **16** Problems Correct _____

28

---

# Answer Key

---

**Name**_____  Skill: Adding Decimals

Add.

| | | | |
|---|---|---|---|
| 1. $\begin{array}{r} 5.6 \\ +\ 2.3 \\ \hline 7.9 \end{array}$ | 2. $\begin{array}{r} 2.5 \\ +\ 8.6 \\ \hline 11.1 \end{array}$ | 3. $\begin{array}{r} 11.5 \\ +\ 3.3 \\ \hline 14.8 \end{array}$ | 4. $\begin{array}{r} 2.6 \\ +\ 7.8 \\ \hline 10.4 \end{array}$ |
| 5. $\begin{array}{r} 21.5 \\ +\ 2.9 \\ \hline 24.4 \end{array}$ | 6. $\begin{array}{r} 38.7 \\ +\ 3.4 \\ \hline 42.1 \end{array}$ | 7. $\begin{array}{r} 94.5 \\ +\ 37.6 \\ \hline 132.1 \end{array}$ | 8. $\begin{array}{r} 80.5 \\ +\ 35.3 \\ \hline 115.8 \end{array}$ |
| 9. $\begin{array}{r} .54 \\ +\ .82 \\ \hline 1.36 \end{array}$ | 10. $\begin{array}{r} 5.78 \\ +\ 5.07 \\ \hline 10.85 \end{array}$ | 11. $\begin{array}{r} 32.52 \\ +\ 12.63 \\ \hline 45.15 \end{array}$ | 12. $\begin{array}{r} 15.87 \\ +\ 77.19 \\ \hline 93.06 \end{array}$ |
| 13. $\begin{array}{r} 2.2 \\ 1.5 \\ +\ 7.7 \\ \hline 11.4 \end{array}$ | 14. $\begin{array}{r} 41.7 \\ 5.2 \\ +\ 2.4 \\ \hline 49.3 \end{array}$ | 15. $\begin{array}{r} 7.1 \\ 18.5 \\ +\ 15.4 \\ \hline 41 \end{array}$ | 16. $\begin{array}{r} 10.12 \\ 10.27 \\ +\ 90.33 \\ \hline 110.72 \end{array}$ |
| 17. $\begin{array}{r} 2.456 \\ 3.088 \\ +\ 8.645 \\ \hline 14.189 \end{array}$ | 18. $\begin{array}{r} 57.00 \\ 87.49 \\ +\ 37.12 \\ \hline 181.61 \end{array}$ | 19. $\begin{array}{r} 212.6 \\ 422.3 \\ +\ 223.7 \\ \hline 858.6 \end{array}$ | 20. $\begin{array}{r} 4.022 \\ 1.341 \\ +\ .037 \\ \hline 5.400 \end{array}$ |

Total Problems _20_  Problems Correct ____

---

**Name**_____  Skill: Adding Decimals

Add.

| | | | |
|---|---|---|---|
| 1. $\begin{array}{r} 3.35 \\ .01 \\ +\ 4.60 \\ \hline 7.96 \end{array}$ | 2. $\begin{array}{r} 33.87 \\ 45.88 \\ +\ 1.12 \\ \hline 80.87 \end{array}$ | 3. $\begin{array}{r} .255 \\ 1.70 \\ +\ 23.15 \\ \hline 25.105 \end{array}$ | 4. $\begin{array}{r} .3 \\ 4.2 \\ +\ .22 \\ \hline 4.72 \end{array}$ |
| 5. $\begin{array}{r} 221.7 \\ 3.35 \\ +\ .07 \\ \hline 225.12 \end{array}$ | 6. $\begin{array}{r} 317.5 \\ 1.4 \\ +\ 88.4 \\ \hline 407.3 \end{array}$ | 7. $\begin{array}{r} 24.15 \\ .15 \\ +\ 5.67 \\ \hline 29.97 \end{array}$ | 8. $\begin{array}{r} 1.88 \\ 22.03 \\ +\ .09 \\ \hline 24.00 \end{array}$ |
| 9. $\begin{array}{r} 12.56 \\ 73.38 \\ +\ .08 \\ \hline 86.02 \end{array}$ | 10. $\begin{array}{r} 5.14 \\ .027 \\ +\ 72.5 \\ \hline 77.667 \end{array}$ | 11. $\begin{array}{r} 5.1 \\ 7.80 \\ +\ 80.4 \\ \hline 93.30 \end{array}$ | 12. $\begin{array}{r} 4.5 \\ 5.4 \\ +\ 12.97 \\ \hline 22.87 \end{array}$ |

13. $12.7 + .13 + 1.2 = 14.03$

14. $.735 + 6.55 + 13 = 20.285$

15. $31.5 + 1.2 + 571.35 = 604.05$

16. $42 + .522 + 7.2 = 49.722$

Total Problems _16_  Problems Correct ____

---

**Name**_____  Skill: Adding Decimals

Add.

1. $1.429 + 21.8 = 23.229$

2. $.9 + .85 = 1.75$

3. $5.15 + 17.623 = 22.773$

4. $52.14 + 12.7 = 64.84$

5. $.911 + 3.2 = 4.111$

6. $46.25 + 12.56 = 58.81$

7. $1.654 + 2.511 = 4.165$

8. $1.23 + 1.654 = 2.884$

9. $81.75 + 23.55 = 105.3$

10. $7.521 + 2.1 = 9.621$

11. $21.2 + .231 = 21.431$

12. $68.58 + .925 = 69.505$

13. $16.68 + 23.665 = 40.345$

14. $1.522 + 8.2 = 9.722$

15. $88.17 + 26.5 = 114.67$

16. $3.901 + 39.01 = 42.911$

Total Problems _16_  Problems Correct ____

---

**Name**_____  Skill: Adding Decimals

Add.

1. $12.4 + 2.689 = 15.089$

2. $.006 + 1.4 = 1.406$

3. $18.529 + 4.5 = 23.029$

4. $23.09 + 16 = 39.09$

5. $18.4 + .06 = 18.46$

6. $.023 + 23.4 = 23.423$

7. $3.49 + 8.9 = 12.39$

8. $.024 + 73.5 = 73.524$

9. $123.4 + 12.2 = 135.6$

10. $23.1 + 16.902 = 40.002$

11. $56.1 + 26.49 = 82.59$

12. $5.01 + 273.4 = 278.41$

13. $.007 + 8.32 = 8.327$

14. $17.829 + 2.2 = 20.029$

15. $.52 + .049 = .569$

16. $75.23 + 26.01 = 101.24$

Total Problems _16_  Problems Correct ____

---

# Answer Key

---

Name_____    Skill: Subtracting Decimals

Subtract.

| | | | |
|---|---|---|---|
| 1. .7<br>− .2<br>.5 | 2. .8<br>− .3<br>.5 | 3. .6<br>− .2<br>.4 | 4. .9<br>− .5<br>.4 |
| 5. .45<br>− .21<br>.24 | 6. .77<br>− .25<br>.52 | 7. .24<br>− .15<br>.09 | 8. .50<br>− .11<br>.39 |
| 9. .885<br>− .325<br>.560 | 10. .987<br>− .521<br>.466 | 11. .608<br>− .321<br>.287 | 12. .952<br>− .335<br>.617 |
| 13. 19.6<br>− 2.1<br>17.5 | 14. 22.6<br>− .2<br>22.4 | 15. 71.6<br>− .7<br>70.9 | 16. 39.99<br>− 3.72<br>36.27 |
| 17. 80.15<br>− .32<br>79.83 | 18. 95.33<br>− 5.21<br>90.12 | 19. 88.43<br>− 12.03<br>76.40 | 20. 61.91<br>− 3.41<br>58.50 |

Total Problems 20  Problems Correct ____

© Carson-Dellosa CD-3750      33

---

Name_____    Skill: Subtracting Decimals

Subtract.

| | | | |
|---|---|---|---|
| 1. 15.867<br>− 4.27<br>11.597 | 2. 30.322<br>− .51<br>29.812 | 3. 21.423<br>− 1.2<br>20.223 | 4. 62.456<br>− 4.2<br>58.256 |
| 5. 4.31<br>− .4<br>3.91 | 6. 826.83<br>− 22.5<br>804.33 | 7. 91.35<br>− 2.672<br>88.678 | 8. 91.384<br>− 2.788<br>88.596 |
| 9. 6.224<br>− 3.04<br>3.184 | 10. 30.9<br>− 5.21<br>25.69 | 11. 81.1<br>− 2.652<br>78.448 | 12. 54.75<br>− 6.213<br>48.537 |

13. 43.154 − 2.08 =  41.074     14. .45 − .224 =  .226

15. .9 − .832 =  .068     16. 3.3 − 1.657 =  1.643

Total Problems 16  Problems Correct ____

© Carson-Dellosa CD-3750      34

---

Name_____    Skill: Multiplying Decimals

Multiply.

| | | | |
|---|---|---|---|
| 1. .2<br>x 5<br>1.0 | 2. .3<br>x 6<br>1.8 | 3. .4<br>x .1<br>.04 | 4. .7<br>x .8<br>.56 |
| 5. .09<br>x 2<br>.18 | 6. .06<br>x 5<br>.30 | 7. 4<br>x .12<br>.48 | 8. 3<br>x .25<br>.75 |
| 9. 9.5<br>x 3<br>28.5 | 10. 5.5<br>x 2<br>11.0 | 11. 3.56<br>x 6<br>21.36 | 12. 5.66<br>x .8<br>4.528 |
| 13. .22<br>x .23<br>.0506 | 14. 7.8<br>x 5.4<br>42.12 | 15. .15<br>x .21<br>.0315 | 16. 1.5<br>x 3.1<br>4.65 |
| 17. .86<br>x 5.4<br>4.644 | 18. 4.1<br>x 5.5<br>22.55 | 19. .07<br>x 12<br>.84 | 20. 32<br>x 5.4<br>172.8 |

Total Problems 20  Problems Correct ____

© Carson-Dellosa CD-3750      35

---

Name_____    Skill: Multiplying Decimals

Multiply.

| | | | |
|---|---|---|---|
| 1. .231<br>x 1.3<br>.3003 | 2. 6.42<br>x 2.3<br>14.766 | 3. 7.41<br>x .9<br>6.669 | 4. 5.11<br>x .51<br>2.6061 |
| 5. .611<br>x 110<br>67.21 | 6. 23.7<br>x 13.5<br>319.95 | 7. 16.2<br>x 34.7<br>562.14 | 8. 8.22<br>x .852<br>7.00344 |
| 9. .888<br>x .402<br>.356976 | 10. 325.5<br>x 54.7<br>17,804.85 | 11. 78.45<br>x 7.26<br>569.547 | 12. 3.365<br>x .32<br>1.0768 |

13. 27.556 x 85.4 = 2,353.2824     14. .623 x 5.07 = 3.15861

15. 3.850 x 905.7 = 3,486.945     16. 55.4 x .657 = 36.3978

Total Problems 16  Problems Correct ____

© Carson-Dellosa CD-3750      36

---

# Answer Key

## Page 37

Name_____    Skill: Multiplying Decimals

Multiply.

1.  .112
   x 1.4
   .1568

2.  8.56
   x 2.1
   17.976

3.  3.66
   x .7
   2.562

4.  8.24
   x .71
   5.8504

5.  2.22
   x 1.2
   2.664

6.  88.4
   x 13.5
   1193.4

7.  18.7
   x 12.9
   241.23

8.  9.32
   x .652
   6.07664

9.  .752
   x .366
   .275232

10. 119.5
   x 24.7
   2951.65

11. 44.45
   x 7.81
   347.1545

12. 3.206
   x .71
   2.27626

13. 37.899 x 23.8 = 901.9962

14. .611 x 5.20 = 3.1772

15. 3.731 x 444.7 = 1659.1757

16. 51.4 x .132 = 6.7848

Total Problems 16   Problems Correct ____

© Carson-Dellosa CD-3750

37

## Page 38

Name_____    Skill: Dividing Decimals

Divide.

1.  $8\overline{)3.2} = .4$
2.  $6\overline{)6.0} = 1$
3.  $3\overline{)3.6} = 1.20$
4.  $6\overline{).24} = .04$
5.  $7\overline{)3.5} = .50$

6.  $3\overline{)2.7} = .9$
7.  $8\overline{).88} = .11$
8.  $4\overline{).36} = .09$
9.  $4\overline{).12} = .03$
10. $9\overline{)4.5} = .50$

11. $5\overline{).30} = .06$
12. $8\overline{).48} = .06$
13. $.02\overline{)56} = 2800$
14. $.7\overline{)84} = 120$
15. $.03\overline{)42} = 1400$

16. $.6\overline{)54} = 90$
17. $.08\overline{)5.6} = 70$
18. $.5\overline{)6.0} = 12$
19. $.2\overline{).18} = .90$
20. $.4\overline{)2.8} = 7$

Total Problems 20   Problems Correct ____

© Carson-Dellosa CD-3750

38

## Page 39

Name_____    Skill: Dividing Decimals

Divide. Round answers to the thousandths.

1.  $5\overline{)6.0} = 1.2$
2.  $.12\overline{)36} = 300$
3.  $.3\overline{)15} = 50$
4.  $.04\overline{)1.20} = 30$

5.  $.3\overline{)3.15} = 10.5$
6.  $2.2\overline{)7.04} = 3.2$
7.  $3\overline{).360} = .12$
8.  $4.4\overline{)27.72} = 6.3$

9.  $15\overline{)30.60} = 2.04$
10. $1.5\overline{)1.50} = 1.0$
11. $.20\overline{)700} = 3500$
12. $.5\overline{)15.55} = 31.1$

13. $1.9\overline{)38.38} = 20.2$
14. $.06\overline{).306} = 5.10$
15. $5.2\overline{)18.72} = 3.60$
16. $6.6\overline{)15.18} = 2.30$

Total Problems 16   Problems Correct ____

© Carson-Dellosa CD-3750

39

## Page 40

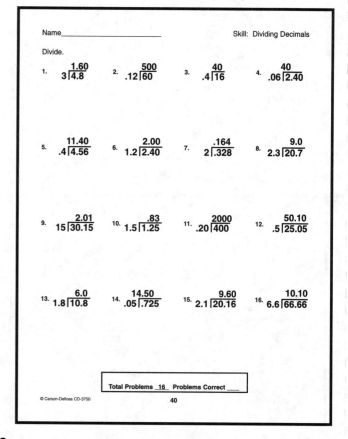

Name_____    Skill: Dividing Decimals

Divide.

1.  $3\overline{)4.8} = 1.60$
2.  $.12\overline{)60} = 500$
3.  $.4\overline{)16} = 40$
4.  $.06\overline{)2.40} = 40$

5.  $.4\overline{)4.56} = 11.40$
6.  $1.2\overline{)2.40} = 2.00$
7.  $2\overline{).328} = .164$
8.  $2.3\overline{)20.7} = 9.0$

9.  $15\overline{)30.15} = 2.01$
10. $1.5\overline{)1.25} = .83$
11. $.20\overline{)400} = 2000$
12. $.5\overline{)25.05} = 50.10$

13. $1.8\overline{)10.8} = 6.0$
14. $.05\overline{).725} = 14.50$
15. $2.1\overline{)20.16} = 9.60$
16. $6.6\overline{)66.66} = 10.10$

Total Problems 16   Problems Correct ____

© Carson-Dellosa CD-3750

40

© Carson-Dellosa CD-3750

106

# Answer Key

---

Name_____  Skill: Changing Percentages to Decimals

Change the following percentages to decimals.

1. **30% = .30**    2. **45% = .45**    3. **60% = .6**    4. **80% = .8**

5. **33% = .33**    6. **20% = .2**    7. **12% = .12**    8. **5% = .05**

9. **13% = .13**    10. **90% = .9**    11. **27% = .27**    12. **110% = 1.1**

13. **34% = .34**    14. **115% = 1.15**    15. **45% = .45**    16. **155% = 1.55**

Total Problems _16_ Problems Correct ____

© Carson-Dellosa CD-3750      41

---

Name_____  Skill: Changing Fractions and Mixed Numbers to Percentages

Change the following fractions and mixed numbers to percentages.

1. $\frac{1}{4}$ = .25    2. $\frac{2}{5}$ = .40    3. $\frac{49}{50}$ = .98    4. $\frac{17}{10}$ = 1.7    5. $\frac{1}{5}$ = .2

6. $\frac{7}{50}$ = .14    7. $\frac{2}{10}$ = .2    8. $\frac{31}{50}$ = .62    9. $\frac{13}{50}$ = .26    10. $\frac{9}{10}$ = .9

11. $\frac{3}{5}$ = .6    12. $\frac{3}{4}$ = .75    13. $\frac{7}{20}$ = .35    14. $\frac{7}{25}$ = .28    15. $\frac{3}{10}$ = .3

16. $1\frac{2}{5}$ = 1.4    17. $3\frac{31}{50}$ = 3.62    18. $1\frac{43}{50}$ = 1.86    19. $4\frac{4}{25}$ = 4.16

20. $4\frac{4}{8}$ = 4.5    21. $5\frac{1}{5}$ = 5.2    22. $4\frac{1}{4}$ = 4.25    23. $2\frac{8}{32}$ = 2.25

Total Problems _23_ Problems Correct ____

© Carson-Dellosa CD-3750      42

---

Name_____  Skill: Changing Decimals to Percentages

Change the following decimals to percentages.

1. **.3 = 30%**    2. **.03 = 3%**    3. **4.03 = 403%**    4. **8.75 = 875%**

5. **87.5 = 8750%**    6. **.34 = 34%**    7. **1.67 = 167%**    8. **15.8 = 1580%**

9. **.04 = 4%**    10. **1.25 = 125%**    11. **.16 = 16%**    12. **1.62 = 162%**

13. **.8 = 80%**    14. **2.5 = 250%**    15. **.375 = 37.5%**    16. **.07 = 7%**

Total Problems _16_ Problems Correct ____

© Carson-Dellosa CD-3750      43

---

Name_____  Skill: Changing Decimals to Percentages

Change the following decimals to percentages.

1. **.59 = 59%**    2. **2.1 = 210%**    3. **63.4 = 6340%**    4. **.4 = 40%**

5. **2.3 = 230%**    6. **.2 = 20%**    7. **5.4 = 540%**    8. **.07 = 7%**

9. **.52 = 52%**    10. **.02 = 2%**    11. **3.34 = 334%**    12. **.061 = 6.1%**

13. **.375 = 37.5%**    14. **.004 = .4%**    15. **2.217 = 221.7%**    16. **.0342 = 3.42%**

Total Problems _16_ Problems Correct ____

© Carson-Dellosa CD-3750      44

---

© Carson-Dellosa CD-3750      **107**

# Answer Key

Name_____    Skill: Finding Percentages

Find the percentages.

1. 17% of 200 = ___34___
2. 25% of 90 = ___22.5___
3. 35% of 50 = ___17.5___
4. 15% of 150 = ___22.5___
5. 85% of 60 = ___51___
6. 65% of 80 = ___52___
7. 10% of 50 = ___5___
8. 100% of 8 = ___8___
9. 32% of 40 = ___12.8___
10. 25% of 30 = ___7.5___
11. 75% of 40 = ___30___
12. 10% of 96 = ___9.6___
13. 60% of 80 = ___48___
14. 12% of 80 = ___9.6___

Total Problems _14_ Problems Correct ___

© Carson-Dellosa CD-3750       45

---

Name_____    Skill: Finding Percentages

Find the percentages.

1. 8% of 180 = ___14.4___
2. 32% of 15 = ___4.8___
3. 80% of 540 = ___432___
4. 25% of 132 = ___33___
5. 25% of 40 = ___10___
6. 1% of 70 = ___.70___
7. 4% of 180 = ___7.2___
8. 120% of 90 = ___108___
9. 33% of 69 = ___22.77___
10. 62% of 48 = ___29.76___
11. 120% of 80 = ___96___
12. 30% of 70 = ___21___
13. 40% of 20 = ___8___
14. 30% of 140 = ___42___

Total Problems _14_ Problems Correct ___

© Carson-Dellosa CD-3750       46

---

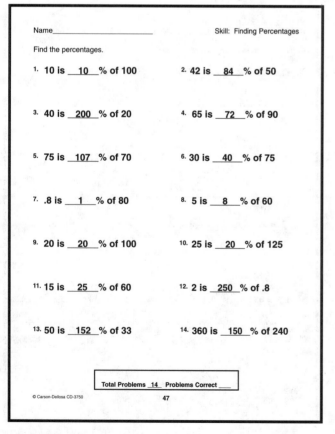

Name_____    Skill: Finding Percentages

Find the percentages.

1. 10 is ___10___% of 100
2. 42 is ___84___% of 50
3. 40 is ___200___% of 20
4. 65 is ___72___% of 90
5. 75 is ___107___% of 70
6. 30 is ___40___% of 75
7. .8 is ___1___% of 80
8. 5 is ___8___% of 60
9. 20 is ___20___% of 100
10. 25 is ___20___% of 125
11. 15 is ___25___% of 60
12. 2 is ___250___% of .8
13. 50 is ___152___% of 33
14. 360 is ___150___% of 240

Total Problems _14_ Problems Correct ___

© Carson-Dellosa CD-3750       47

---

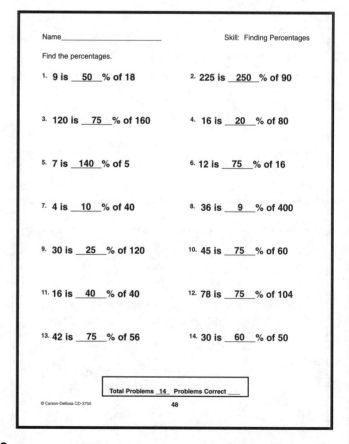

Name_____    Skill: Finding Percentages

Find the percentages.

1. 9 is ___50___% of 18
2. 225 is ___250___% of 90
3. 120 is ___75___% of 160
4. 16 is ___20___% of 80
5. 7 is ___140___% of 5
6. 12 is ___75___% of 16
7. 4 is ___10___% of 40
8. 36 is ___9___% of 400
9. 30 is ___25___% of 120
10. 45 is ___75___% of 60
11. 16 is ___40___% of 40
12. 78 is ___75___% of 104
13. 42 is ___75___% of 56
14. 30 is ___60___% of 50

Total Problems _14_ Problems Correct ___

© Carson-Dellosa CD-3750       48

# Answer Key

---

Name_____    Skill: Finding Percentages

Solve.

1. 18 is 75% of ___24___

2. 5 is 10% of ___50___

3. 4 is 25% of ___16___

4. 70 is 175% of ___40___

5. 9 is 100% of ___9___

6. 60 is 150% of ___40___

7. .7 is 50% of ___1.4___

8. 8 is 4% of ___200___

9. 1 is 25% of ___4___

10. 32 is 50% of ___64___

11. 15 is 50% of ___30___

12. 30 is 10% of ___300___

13. 42 is 40% of ___105___

14. 60 is 200% of ___30___

Total Problems _14_ Problems Correct ____

© Carson-Dellosa CD-3750

49

---

Name_____    Skill: Finding Percentages

Solve.

1. 57 is 150% of ___38___

2. 39 is 52% of ___75___

3. 88 is 110% of ___80___

4. 73 is 20% of ___365___

5. 19 is 25% of ___76___

6. 60 is 150% of ___40___

7. 408 is 85% of ___480___

8. 18 is 25% of ___72___

9. 72 is 80% of ___90___

10. 9 is 30% of ___30___

11. 26 is 52% of ___50___

12. 50 is 40% of ___125___

13. 20 is 50% of ___40___

14. 32 is 80% of ___40___

Total Problems _14_ Problems Correct ____

© Carson-Dellosa CD-3750

50

---

Name_____    Skill: Order of Operations

Solve.

1. (20 − 5) ÷ 3 = 5

2. 12 + (2 + 1) = 15

3. 36 ÷ (3 x 3) = 4

4. 6 ÷ 2 x 3 = 9

5. 125 ÷ (37 − 12) = 5

6. (10 + 10) ÷ 2 = 10

7. (3 x 8) ÷ 8 = 3

8. (42 − 35) x 6 = 42

9. (6 x 3) ÷ 9 = 2

10. (2 + 10) x (8 − 4) = 48

11. (4 x 6) ÷ 12 = 2

12. 30 + (15 ÷ 5) = 33

13. (7 + 5) x 4 = 48

14. (2 x 3 + 12) ÷ 3 = 6

Total Problems _14_ Problems Correct ____

© Carson-Dellosa CD-3750

51

---

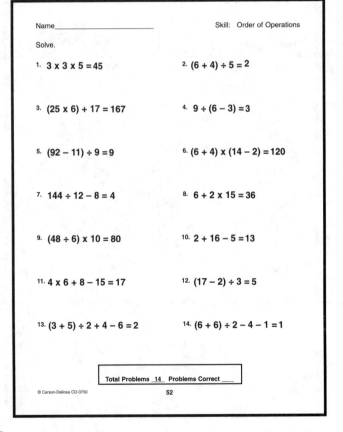

Name_____    Skill: Order of Operations

Solve.

1. 3 x 3 x 5 = 45

2. (6 + 4) ÷ 5 = 2

3. (25 x 6) + 17 = 167

4. 9 ÷ (6 − 3) = 3

5. (92 − 11) ÷ 9 = 9

6. (6 + 4) x (14 − 2) = 120

7. 144 ÷ 12 − 8 = 4

8. 6 + 2 x 15 = 36

9. (48 ÷ 6) x 10 = 80

10. 2 + 16 − 5 = 13

11. 4 x 6 + 8 − 15 = 17

12. (17 − 2) ÷ 3 = 5

13. (3 + 5) ÷ 2 + 4 − 6 = 2

14. (6 + 6) ÷ 2 − 4 − 1 = 1

Total Problems _14_ Problems Correct ____

© Carson-Dellosa CD-3750

52

---

# Answer Key

---

Name_____  Skill: Order of Operations

Solve.

1. $363 \div (7 - 4) = 121$
2. $64 \div (20 - 16) = 16$
3. $(6 + 5) \times 2 + 3 = 25$
4. $12 \times (8 + 4) = 144$
5. $(6 + 2) \times 4 = 32$
6. $2 \times (4 + 10) = 28$
7. $8 - 6 + 12 = 14$
8. $25 \times 3 + 78 = 153$
9. $(24 \div 6) \times 11 = 44$
10. $3 + 18 - 5 = 16$
11. $(2 + 12) \div 7 = 2$
12. $4 \times (17 + 20) = 148$
13. $(42 - 18) \div (10 - 4) = 4$
14. $(3 + 6) \div 3 - 1 - 1 = 1$

Total Problems _14_ Problems Correct ____

53

---

Name_____  Skill: Order of Operations

Solve.

1. $3 \times (16 + 27) = 129$
2. $(2 \times 16) \div 8 = 4$
3. $95 - 6 + 27 = 116$
4. $90 \div (50 - 40) = 9$
5. $32 \div 8 + 8 = 12$
6. $32 \div (8 + 8) = 2$
7. $(7 \times 6) \div 2 = 21$
8. $14 + (1 \times 7) = 21$
9. $(20 \div 5) \times 10 = 40$
10. $4 + 19 - 5 = 18$
11. $(3 + 18) \div 7 = 3$
12. $4 \times (16 + 20) = 144$
13. $(40 - 10) \div (10 - 5) = 6$
14. $4 + 8 \div 3 - 2 - 0 = 2$

Total Problems _14_ Problems Correct ____

© Carson-Dellosa CD-3750
54

---

Name_____  Skill: Adding Integers

Add.

1. $2 + {}^-7 = {}^-5$
2. ${}^-7 + {}^-2 = {}^-9$
3. ${}^-6 + 4 = {}^-2$
4. $9 + {}^-7 = 2$
5. ${}^-4 + 3 = {}^-1$
6. ${}^-3 + {}^-6 = {}^-9$
7. ${}^-1 + {}^-8 = {}^-9$
8. $5 + {}^-6 = {}^-1$
9. $9 + {}^-8 = 1$
10. $11 + {}^-5 = 6$
11. $2 + {}^-4 = {}^-2$
12. $4 + {}^-1 = 3$
13. ${}^-12 + {}^-3 = {}^-15$
14. ${}^-8 + {}^-7 = {}^-15$
15. ${}^-3 + {}^-4 = {}^-7$
16. $8 + {}^-2 = 6$
17. $13 + {}^-1 = 12$
18. ${}^-3 + {}^-4 = {}^-1$

Total Problems _18_ Problems Correct ____

© Carson-Dellosa CD-3750
55

---

Name_____  Skill: Adding Integers

Add.

1. $42 + {}^-18 = 24$
2. ${}^-54 + {}^-87 = {}^-141$
3. ${}^-61 + 40 = {}^-21$
4. $90 + {}^-71 = 19$
5. ${}^-42 + 31 = {}^-11$
6. ${}^-34 + {}^-62 = {}^-96$
7. ${}^-12 + {}^-80 = {}^-92$
8. $15 + {}^-61 = {}^-46$
9. $3 + {}^-42 = {}^-39$
10. $9 + {}^-4 = 5$
11. $22 + {}^-41 = {}^-19$
12. $54 + {}^-1 = 53$
13. ${}^-18 + {}^-3 = {}^-21$
14. ${}^-80 + {}^-79 = {}^-159$
15. ${}^-5 + {}^-6 = {}^-11$
16. $7 + {}^-3 = 4$
17. $14 + {}^-5 = 9$
18. $6 + {}^-8 = {}^-2$

Total Problems _18_ Problems Correct ____

© Carson-Dellosa CD-3750
56

---

© Carson-Dellosa CD-3750
**110**

# Answer Key

---

**Name_____**  Skill: Adding Integers

Add.

1. $45 + {}^-78 = {}^-33$
2. ${}^-27 + {}^-2 = {}^-29$
3. ${}^-46 + 4 = {}^-42$
4. $15 + {}^-72 = {}^-57$
5. ${}^-40 + 35 = {}^-5$
6. ${}^-31 + {}^-61 = {}^-92$
7. ${}^-19 + {}^-82 = {}^-101$
8. $65 + {}^-6 = 59$
9. $48 + {}^-82 = {}^-34$
10. $65 + {}^-56 = 9$
11. $42 + {}^-48 = {}^-6$
12. $18 + {}^-18 = 0$
13. ${}^-18 + {}^-32 = {}^-50$
14. ${}^-17 + {}^-21 = {}^-38$
15. ${}^-32 + {}^-42 = {}^-74$
16. $25 + {}^-25 = 0$
17. $46 + {}^-18 = 28$
18. $25 + {}^-4 = 21$

Total Problems _18_ Problems Correct ____

57

---

**Name_____**  Skill: Adding Integers

Add.

1. ${}^-26 + {}^-16 = {}^-42$
2. ${}^-32 + {}^-15 = {}^-47$
3. ${}^-20 + {}^-30 = {}^-50$
4. $27 + {}^-18 = 9$
5. ${}^-41 + 23 = {}^-18$
6. ${}^-33 + {}^-66 = {}^-99$
7. ${}^-17 + {}^-82 = {}^-99$
8. ${}^-55 + {}^-66 = {}^-121$
9. $91 + {}^-81 = 10$
10. $14 + {}^-3 = 11$
11. $77 + {}^-82 = {}^-5$
12. $44 + {}^-14 = 30$
13. ${}^-62 + {}^-27 = {}^-89$
14. ${}^-51 + {}^-38 = {}^-89$
15. ${}^-23 + {}^-24 = {}^-47$
16. $88 + {}^-35 = 53$
17. $21 + {}^-19 = 2$
18. $33 + {}^-40 = {}^-7$

Total Problems _18_ Problems Correct ____

58

---

**Name_____**  Skill: Subtracting Integers

Subtract.

1. ${}^-2 - 7 = {}^-9$
2. $5 - {}^-7 = 12$
3. ${}^-6 - {}^-10 = 4$
4. $4 - {}^-1 = 5$
5. $4 - {}^-6 = 10$
6. ${}^-8 - {}^-3 = {}^-5$
7. ${}^-8 - {}^-9 = 1$
8. ${}^-3 - {}^-7 = 4$
9. $9 - {}^-8 = 17$
10. $5 - {}^-2 = 7$
11. $4 - {}^-2 = 6$
12. $5 - {}^-3 = 8$
13. ${}^-8 - {}^-4 = {}^-4$
14. ${}^-9 - {}^-3 = {}^-6$
15. ${}^-7 - {}^-9 = 2$
16. $8 - {}^-4 = 12$
17. $13 - {}^-2 = 15$
18. $2 - {}^-3 = 5$

Total Problems _18_ Problems Correct ____

59

---

**Name_____**  Skill: Subtracting Integers

Subtract.

1. ${}^-4 - 5 = {}^-9$
2. ${}^-11 - {}^-3 = {}^-8$
3. ${}^-6 - {}^-2 = {}^-4$
4. $10 - 2 = 8$
5. $2 - {}^-3 = 5$
6. ${}^-6 - {}^-5 = {}^-1$
7. ${}^-3 - {}^-8 = 5$
8. ${}^-4 - {}^-6 = 2$
9. $7 - {}^-8 = 15$
10. $4 - {}^-1 = 5$
11. $5 - {}^-6 = 11$
12. $8 - {}^-2 = 10$
13. ${}^-9 - {}^-3 = {}^-6$
14. ${}^-8 - {}^-6 = {}^-2$
15. ${}^-5 - {}^-3 = {}^-2$
16. $7 - {}^-2 = 9$
17. $10 - {}^-5 = 15$
18. $8 - {}^-3 = 11$

Total Problems _18_ Problems Correct ____

60

---

# Answer Key

---

Name_____  Skill: Subtracting Integers

Subtract.

1. $^-27 - 14 = {}^-41$ 2. $^-22 - {}^-32 = 10$ 3. $^-26 - {}^-41 = 15$

4. $50 - 30 = 20$ 5. $17 - {}^-16 = 33$ 6. $^-18 - {}^-24 = 6$

7. $^-23 - {}^-42 = 19$ 8. $^-21 - {}^-35 = 14$ 9. $17 - {}^-20 = 37$

10. $35 - {}^-16 = 51$ 11. $25 - {}^-25 = 50$ 12. $39 - {}^-42 = 81$

13. $^-85 - {}^-75 = {}^-10$ 14. $^-46 - {}^-27 = {}^-19$ 15. $^-88 - {}^-92 = 4$

16. $39 - {}^-62 = 101$ 17. $47 - {}^-64 = 111$ 18. $47 - {}^-53 = 100$

Total Problems _18_ Problems Correct ____

© Carson-Dellosa CD-3750
61

---

Name_____  Skill: Subtracting Integers

Subtract.

1. $^-42 - 34 = {}^-76$ 2. $^-56 - {}^-77 = 21$ 3. $^-50 - {}^-62 = 12$

4. $30 - {}^-20 = 50$ 5. $^-48 - {}^-52 = 4$ 6. $^-78 - {}^-34 = {}^-44$

7. $^-83 - {}^-62 = {}^-21$ 8. $^-24 - {}^-55 = 31$ 9. $37 - {}^-50 = 87$

10. $52 - {}^-38 = 90$ 11. $45 - {}^-37 = 82$ 12. $29 - {}^-33 = 62$

13. $^-70 - {}^-70 = 0$ 14. $^-26 - {}^-28 = 2$ 15. $^-68 - {}^-90 = 22$

16. $69 - {}^-42 = 111$ 17. $37 - {}^-60 = 97$ 18. $57 - {}^-52 = 109$

Total Problems _18_ Problems Correct ____

© Carson-Dellosa CD-3750
62

---

Name_____  Skill: Adding and Subtracting Integers

Solve.

1. $^-42 - 34 + 15 = {}^-61$ 2. $^-22 - {}^-77 + 12 = 67$

3. $1 + 15 - {}^-4 = 20$ 4. $30 - {}^-15 + {}^-14 = 31$

5. $^-8 - {}^-4 + 5 = 1$ 6. $^-13 - {}^-50 + 16 = 53$

7. $36 - {}^-21 - 12 = 45$ 8. $^-36 - {}^-37 + 23 = 24$

9. $^-40 + {}^-60 - 13 = {}^-113$ 10. $^-51 - {}^-47 + {}^-5 = {}^-9$

11. $^-14 + {}^-10 + 4 = {}^-20$ 12. $21 - {}^-35 + 66 = 122$

Total Problems _12_ Problems Correct ____

© Carson-Dellosa CD-3750
63

---

Name_____  Skill: Adding and Subtracting Integers

Solve.

1. $^-2 - 2 + 2 = {}^-2$ 2. $^-13 - {}^-14 + 10 = 11$

3. $36 + 14 - {}^-31 = 81$ 4. $21 - {}^-26 + {}^-44 = 3$

5. $^-24 - {}^-31 + 19 = 26$ 6. $^-16 - {}^-42 + 31 = 57$

7. $21 - {}^-18 - 25 = 14$ 8. $^-56 - {}^-45 + 3 = {}^-8$

9. $^-21 + {}^-50 - 43 = {}^-114$ 10. $^-13 - {}^-12 + {}^-10 = {}^-11$

11. $^-16 + {}^-12 + 5 = {}^-23$ 12. $17 - {}^-22 + 18 = 57$

Total Problems _12_ Problems Correct ____

© Carson-Dellosa CD-3750
64

---

© Carson-Dellosa CD-3750   112

# Answer Key

**113**

---

## Worksheet (page 65)

Name_____     Skill: Multiplying Integers

Multiply.

1. $^-3 \times 2 = {}^-6$
2. $^-6 \times 3 = {}^-18$
3. $^-5 \times {}^-7 = 35$
4. $9 \times {}^-3 = {}^-27$
5. $^-6 \times {}^-4 = 24$
6. $2 \times {}^-10 = {}^-20$
7. $^-3 \times 8 = {}^-24$
8. $^-3 \times 7 = {}^-21$
9. $^-6 \times {}^-2 = 12$
10. $21 \times {}^-25 = {}^-525$
11. $^-10 \times {}^-3 = 30$
12. $^-2 \times 9 = {}^-18$
13. $^-5 \times 3 = {}^-15$
14. $^-9 \times {}^-6 = 54$
15. $^-7 \times 3 = {}^-21$
16. $^-16 \times 2 = {}^-32$
17. $2 \times {}^-18 = {}^-36$
18. $6 \times {}^-2 = {}^-12$

Total Problems _18_ Problems Correct ____

© Carson-Dellosa CD-3750     65

---

## Worksheet (page 66)

Name_____     Skill: Multiplying Integers

Multiply.

1. $^-5 \times 11 = {}^-55$
2. $^-7 \times 2 = {}^-14$
3. $^-8 \times {}^-4 = 32$
4. $6 \times {}^-5 = {}^-30$
5. $^-8 \times {}^-2 = 16$
6. $3 \times {}^-12 = {}^-36$
7. $^-5 \times 9 = {}^-45$
8. $^-4 \times 8 = {}^-32$
9. $^-7 \times {}^-9 = 63$
10. $18 \times {}^-4 = {}^-72$
11. $^-12 \times {}^-2 = 24$
12. $^-4 \times 7 = {}^-28$
13. $^-6 \times 8 = {}^-48$
14. $^-4 \times {}^-6 = 24$
15. $^-3 \times 3 = {}^-9$
16. $^-6 \times 2 = {}^-12$
17. $2 \times {}^-5 = {}^-10$
18. $0 \times {}^-2 = 0$

Total Problems _18_ Problems Correct ____

© Carson-Dellosa CD-3750     66

---

## Worksheet (page 67)

Name_____     Skill: Multiplying Integers

Multiply.

1. $^-42 \times 20 = {}^-840$
2. $^-18 \times 12 = {}^-216$
3. $^-23 \times {}^-62 = 1,426$
4. $21 \times {}^-4 = {}^-84$
5. $^-33 \times {}^-11 = 363$
6. $9 \times {}^-15 = {}^-135$
7. $^-16 \times 15 = {}^-240$
8. $^-12 \times 13 = {}^-156$
9. $^-20 \times {}^-100 = 2,000$
10. $16 \times {}^-10 = {}^-160$
11. $^-15 \times {}^-30 = 450$
12. $^-2 \times 17 = {}^-34$
13. $^-9 \times 18 = {}^-162$
14. $^-22 \times {}^-16 = 352$
15. $^-18 \times 4 = {}^-72$
16. $^-30 \times 14 = {}^-420$
17. $12 \times {}^-5 = {}^-60$
18. $30 \times {}^-6 = {}^-180$

Total Problems _18_ Problems Correct ____

© Carson-Dellosa CD-3750     67

---

## Worksheet (page 68)

Name_____     Skill: Multiplying Integers

Multiply.

1. $^-20 \times 10 = {}^-200$
2. $^-15 \times 17 = {}^-255$
3. $^-43 \times {}^-60 = 2,580$
4. $14 \times {}^-2 = {}^-28$
5. $^-35 \times {}^-15 = 525$
6. $5 \times {}^-16 = {}^-80$
7. $^-17 \times 2 = {}^-34$
8. $^-9 \times 23 = {}^-207$
9. $^-21 \times {}^-12 = 252$
10. $15 \times {}^-8 = {}^-120$
11. $^-6 \times {}^-21 = 126$
12. $^-20 \times 27 = {}^-540$
13. $^-5 \times 28 = {}^-140$
14. $^-13 \times {}^-12 = 156$
15. $^-15 \times 2 = {}^-30$
16. $^-11 \times 16 = {}^-176$
17. $10 \times {}^-3 = {}^-30$
18. $21 \times {}^-6 = {}^-126$

Total Problems _18_ Problems Correct ____

© Carson-Dellosa CD-3750     68

# Answer Key

---

Name_____

Skill: Multiplying Integers

Multiply.

1. $^{-}5 \times 15 = {}^{-}75$  2. $^{-}21 \times 32 = {}^{-}672$  3. $^{-}18 \times {}^{-}27 = 486$

4. $21 \times {}^{-}16 = {}^{-}336$  5. $^{-}30 \times {}^{-}22 = 660$  6. $3 \times {}^{-}90 = {}^{-}270$

7. $^{-}10 \times 3 = {}^{-}30$  8. $^{-}8 \times 11 = {}^{-}88$  9. $^{-}15 \times {}^{-}17 = 255$

10. $12 \times {}^{-}7 = {}^{-}84$  11. $^{-}4 \times {}^{-}22 = 88$  12. $^{-}21 \times 30 = {}^{-}630$

13. $^{-}8 \times 22 = {}^{-}176$  14. $^{-}15 \times {}^{-}14 = 210$  15. $^{-}13 \times 3 = {}^{-}39$

16. $^{-}10 \times 14 = {}^{-}140$  17. $12 \times {}^{-}6 = {}^{-}72$  18. $31 \times {}^{-}24 = {}^{-}744$

Total Problems _18_ Problems Correct ____

69

---

Name_____

Skill: Substitution

Complete the following.

1. If t = 3, then 12 + t = ___15___

2. If u = 5, then 25 ÷ u = ___5___

3. If w = 4, then 10 − w = ___6___

4. If z = 5, then 11 x z = ___55___

5. If e = 9, then 6 + e = ___15___

6. If g = 2, then 4 ÷ g = ___2___

7. If q = 1, then q + 7 = ___8___

8. If s = 4, then 12 − s = ___8___

9. If k = 14, then 2 x k = ___28___

Total Problems _9_ Problems Correct ____

70

---

Name_____

Skill: Substitution

Complete the following.

1. If r = 6, then 10 + r = ___16___

2. If c = 3, then 24 ÷ c = ___8___

3. If x = 7, then 7 − x = ___0___

4. If a = 4, then 10 x a = ___40___

5. If f = 8, then 21 + f = ___29___

6. If g = 3, then 9 ÷ g = ___3___

7. If q = 8, then q + 9 = ___17___

8. If m = 3, then 10 − m = ___7___

9. If p = 16, then 1 x p = ___16___

Total Problems _9_ Problems Correct ____

71

---

Name_____

Skill: Substitution

Complete the following.

1. If r = 2, then 15 + r = ___17___

2. If c = 12, then 36 ÷ c = ___3___

3. If x = 15, then 28 − x = ___13___

4. If a = 19, then 2 x a = ___38___

5. If f = 12, then 20 + f = ___32___

6. If g = 9, then 81 ÷ g = ___9___

7. If q = 16, then 23 + q = ___39___

8. If m = 21, then 35 − m = ___14___

9. If p = 18, then 3 x p = ___54___

Total Problems _9_ Problems Correct ____

72

---

# Answer Key

Name_____  Skill: Substituting the Value of
                                        One Variable

Complete the following.

1.  If r = 5, then 15 + r = ____20____

2.  If h = 15, then 45 ÷ h = ____3____

3.  If e = 31, then 88 − e = ____57____

4.  If n = 14, then 9 + n = ____23____

5.  If k = 41, then 15 + k = ____56____

6.  If p = 4, then 16 ÷ p = ____4____

7.  If w = 12, then 24 + w = ____36____

8.  If v = 35, then 36 − v = ____1____

9.  If s = 7, then 4 x s = ____28____

Total Problems _9_ Problems Correct ____

© Carson-Dellosa CD-3750
73

---

Name_____  Skill: Substitution

Complete the folllowing.

1.  If w = 5, then 18 + w = ____23____

2.  If u = 13, then 39 ÷ u = ____3____

3.  If e = 77, then 95 − e = ____18____

4.  If y = 9, then 8 + y = ____17____

5.  If r = 12, then 0 + r = ____12____

6.  If t = 2, then 32 ÷ t = ____16____

7.  If z = 15, then 21 + z = ____36____

8.  If c = 16, then 42 − c = ____26____

9.  If g = 9, then 5 x g = ____45____

Total Problems _9_ Problems Correct ____

© Carson-Dellosa CD-3750
74

---

Name_____  Skill: Substitution

Solve using the following values: a = 2, b = 3, c = 4, d = 5

1.  a + 4 = 6       2.  3c = 12        3.  c + 15 = 19

4.  b x d = 15      5.  d − a = 3      6.  b + a = 5

7.  3b = 9          8.  a + 20 = 22    9.  4c = 16

10. 5 − a = 3       11. 8 + c = 12     12. b + d = 8

13. a x b = 6       14. 2d = 10        15. 15 + a = 17

16. 30 + b = 33     17. c + b = 7      18. b x c = 12

Total Problems _18_ Problems Correct ____

© Carson-Dellosa CD-3750
75

---

Name_____  Skill: Substituting the Value of One
                                        or Two Variables

Solve using the following values: a = 2, b = 5, c = 10

1.  2c = 20         2.  b + 4 = 9      3.  a + b = 7

4.  c + 10 = 20     5.  8 − b = 3      6.  b + b = 10

7.  3b = 15         8.  b + 20 = 25    9.  4c = 40

10. 30 − c = 20     11. 6b = 30        12. bc = 50

13. c − a = 8       14. 9c = 90        15. 15 + a = 17

16. 4 + a = 6       17. c + 12 = 22    18. 3b = 15

Total Problems _18_ Problems Correct ____

© Carson-Dellosa CD-3750
76

---

# Answer Key

1. $j \div f = 2$
2. $j \times j = 144$
3. $2f = 12$
4. $22 - f = 16$
5. $16i = 160$
6. $16 + g = 24$
7. $24 - g = 16$
8. $f \times i = 60$
9. $4f = 24$
10. $g \times i = 80$
11. $10j = 120$
12. $g \times j = 96$
13. $100 \div i = 10$
14. $18 - j = 6$
15. $7 + f = 13$
16. $j - 6 = 6$
17. $j - f = 6$
18. $24 \div f = 4$

Total Problems _18_ Problems Correct ____

© Carson-Dellosa CD-3750    77

---

Name_____      Skill: Substitution

Solve using the following values: **k = 4, m = 6, n = 8, p = 10**

1. $2k + 4m = 32$
2. $4n \times p = 320$
3. $2p = 20$
4. $10n - p = 70$
5. $km \div 12 = 2$
6. $k + m = 10$
7. $np - 4 = 76$
8. $2m + p = 22$
9. $p - k = 6$
10. $4p - 2n = 24$
11. $8n + m = 70$
12. $pk = 40$
13. $np + 10 = 90$
14. $87 - np = 7$
15. $2p + 2n = 36$
16. $n - 6 = 2$
17. $m - 1 = 5$
18. $3mp = 180$

Total Problems _18_ Problems Correct ____

© Carson-Dellosa CD-3750    78

---

Name_____      Skill: Substitution

Solve using the following values: **r = 3, s = 4, t = 5, u = 6**

1. $2r + s = 10$
2. $4s \times 10 = 160$
3. $2u = 12$
4. $5u - 20 = 10$
5. $2u \div r = 4$
6. $st = 20$
7. $ru - 2t = 8$
8. $u + 2t = 16$
9. $5r - s = 11$
10. $3s \times r = 36$
11. $u \div r = 2$
12. $2u + 4r = 24$
13. $6t + r = 33$
14. $2r - 3 = 3$
15. $t + u = 11$
16. $s \times 3r = 36$
17. $u - 1 = 5$
18. $3tu = 90$

Total Problems _18_ Problems Correct ____

© Carson-Dellosa CD-3750    79

---

Name_____      Skill: Solving Equations

Find the value of each variable.

1. $5 + x = 8$   $x = 3$
2. $4 = y - 16$   $y = 20$
3. $x - 6 = 8$   $x = 14$
4. $14 = 8 + x$   $x = 6$
5. $22 = a + 6$   $a = 16$
6. $3 + x = 4$   $x = 1$
7. $a + 16 = 37$   $a = 21$
8. $25 - y = 5$   $y = 20$
9. $35 = 60 - y$   $y = 25$
10. $y - 4 = 25$   $y = 29$
11. $16 - n = 9$   $n = 7$
12. $b + 5 = 42$   $b = 37$
13. $7 + c = 14$   $c = 7$
14. $28 - d = 12$   $d = 16$
15. $14 + f = 22$   $f = 8$
16. $a - 10 = 6$   $a = 16$
17. $12 + e = 46$   $e = 34$
18. $x + 14 = 16$   $x = 2$

Total Problems _18_ Problems Correct ____

© Carson-Dellosa CD-3750    80

# Answer Key

Name_____     Skill: Solving Equations

Find the value of each variable.

1. $25 + a = 37$
$a = 12$

2. $10 = a + 5$
$a = 5$

3. $x - 9 = 16$
$x = 25$

4. $30 = 7 + x$
$x = 23$

5. $45 = j + 17$
$j = 28$

6. $3 + x = 15$
$x = 12$

7. $a + 12 = 44$
$a = 32$

8. $30 - y = 6$
$y = 24$

9. $25 = 20 - y$
$y = {}^-5$

10. $y - 9 = 16$
$y = 25$

11. $14 - n = 2$
$n = 12$

12. $t + 18 = 56$
$t = 38$

13. $7 + e = 19$
$c = 12$

14. $39 - r = 11$
$r = 28$

15. $89 + n = 100$
$n = 11$

16. $w - 15 = 7$
$w = 22$

17. $13 + p = 23$
$p = 10$

18. $a + 19 = 22$
$a = 3$

Total Problems _18_ Problems Correct ____

© Carson-Dellosa CD-3750     81

---

Name_____     Skill: Solving Equations

Find the value of each variable.

1. $4 + x = 8$
$x = 4$

2. $3 = y - 17$
$y = 20$

3. $x + 6 = 10$
$x = 4$

4. $27 = 9 \times k$
$k = 3$

5. $23 = y + 9$
$y = 14$

6. $5 + e = 50$
$e = 45$

7. $a + 13 = 41$
$a = 28$

8. $30 - h = 9$
$h = 21$

9. $75 = 90 - z$
$z = 15$

10. $y - 2 = 47$
$y = 49$

11. $18 - v = 6$
$v = 12$

12. $s + 4 = 15$
$s = 11$

13. $8 + r = 22$
$r = 14$

14. $31 - d = 10$
$d = 21$

15. $12 \times f = 144$
$f = 12$

16. $\frac{x}{4} = 5$
$x = 20$

17. $\frac{20}{c} = 5$
$c = 4$

18. $\frac{x}{3} = 9$
$x = 27$

Total Problems _18_ Problems Correct ____

© Carson-Dellosa CD-3750     82

---

Name_____     Skill: Solving Equations

Find the value of each variable.

1. $4r = 20$
$r = 5$

2. $15 = 5a$
$a = 3$

3. $2a - 20 = 10$
$a = 15$

4. $80 = 11 + m$
$m = 69$

5. $42 = a + 7$
$a = 35$

6. $52 + t = 98$
$t = 46$

7. $w + 36 = 39$
$w = 3$

8. $75 - q = 0$
$q = 75$

9. $21 = 40 - h$
$h = 19$

10. $a - 44 = 20$
$a = 64$

11. $12 \times n = 72$
$n = 6$

12. $w \times 5 = 60$
$w = 12$

13. $50 - c = 2$
$c = 48$

14. $38 - e = 12$
$e = 26$

15. $15 \times w = 15$
$w = 1$

16. $\frac{c}{9} = 4$
$c = 36$

17. $\frac{33}{c} = 3$
$c = 11$

18. $\frac{r}{6} = 3$
$r = 18$

Total Problems _18_ Problems Correct ____

© Carson-Dellosa CD-3750     83

---

Name_____     Skill: Exponents

Find the squares.

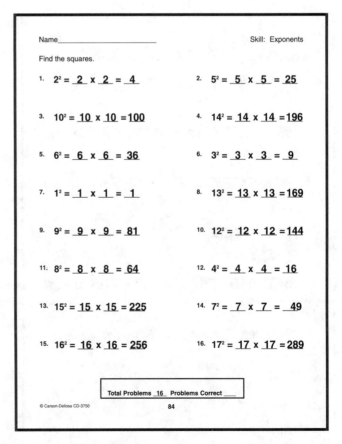

1. $2^2 = \underline{2} \times \underline{2} = \underline{4}$

2. $5^2 = \underline{5} \times \underline{5} = \underline{25}$

3. $10^2 = \underline{10} \times \underline{10} = \underline{100}$

4. $14^2 = \underline{14} \times \underline{14} = \underline{196}$

5. $6^2 = \underline{6} \times \underline{6} = \underline{36}$

6. $3^2 = \underline{3} \times \underline{3} = \underline{9}$

7. $1^2 = \underline{1} \times \underline{1} = \underline{1}$

8. $13^2 = \underline{13} \times \underline{13} = \underline{169}$

9. $9^2 = \underline{9} \times \underline{9} = \underline{81}$

10. $12^2 = \underline{12} \times \underline{12} = \underline{144}$

11. $8^2 = \underline{8} \times \underline{8} = \underline{64}$

12. $4^2 = \underline{4} \times \underline{4} = \underline{16}$

13. $15^2 = \underline{15} \times \underline{15} = \underline{225}$

14. $7^2 = \underline{7} \times \underline{7} = \underline{49}$

15. $16^2 = \underline{16} \times \underline{16} = \underline{256}$

16. $17^2 = \underline{17} \times \underline{17} = \underline{289}$

Total Problems _16_ Problems Correct ____

© Carson-Dellosa CD-3750     84

# Answer Key

---

Name_____     Skill: Exponents

Find the squares.

1. $2^2 = 4$
2. $20^2 = 400$
3. $12^2 = 144$
4. $6^2 = 36$

5. $13^2 = 169$
6. $3^2 = 9$
7. $17^2 = 289$
8. $22^2 = 484$

9. $16^2 = 256$
10. $14^2 = 196$
11. $4^2 = 16$
12. $21^2 = 441$

13. $5^2 = 25$
14. $10^2 = 100$
15. $7^2 = 49$
16. $15^2 = 225$

Total Problems _16_ Problems Correct ___

---

Name_____     Skill: Exponents

Find the squares.

1. $15^2 = 225$
2. $7^2 = 49$
3. $6^2 = 36$
4. $3^2 = 9$

5. $17^2 = 289$
6. $1^2 = 1$
7. $12^2 = 144$
8. $18^2 = 324$

9. $4^2 = 16$
10. $50^2 = 2,500$
11. $30^2 = 900$
12. $13^2 = 169$

13. $40^2 = 1,600$
14. $5^2 = 25$
15. $11^2 = 121$
16. $9^2 = 81$

Total Problems _16_ Problems Correct ___

---

Name_____     Skill: Square Roots

Find the square roots.

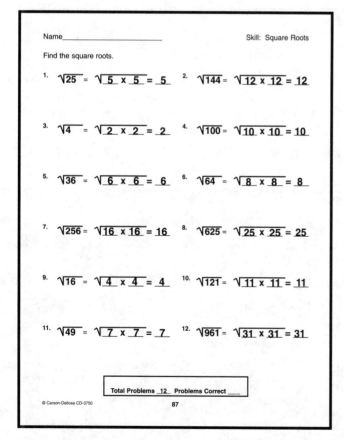

1. $\sqrt{25} = \sqrt{5 \times 5} = 5$
2. $\sqrt{144} = \sqrt{12 \times 12} = 12$

3. $\sqrt{4} = \sqrt{2 \times 2} = 2$
4. $\sqrt{100} = \sqrt{10 \times 10} = 10$

5. $\sqrt{36} = \sqrt{6 \times 6} = 6$
6. $\sqrt{64} = \sqrt{8 \times 8} = 8$

7. $\sqrt{256} = \sqrt{16 \times 16} = 16$
8. $\sqrt{625} = \sqrt{25 \times 25} = 25$

9. $\sqrt{16} = \sqrt{4 \times 4} = 4$
10. $\sqrt{121} = \sqrt{11 \times 11} = 11$

11. $\sqrt{49} = \sqrt{7 \times 7} = 7$
12. $\sqrt{961} = \sqrt{31 \times 31} = 31$

Total Problems _12_ Problems Correct ___

---

Name_____     Skill: Square Roots

Find the square roots.

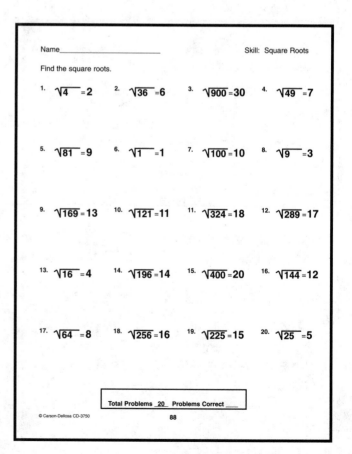

1. $\sqrt{4} = 2$
2. $\sqrt{36} = 6$
3. $\sqrt{900} = 30$
4. $\sqrt{49} = 7$

5. $\sqrt{81} = 9$
6. $\sqrt{1} = 1$
7. $\sqrt{100} = 10$
8. $\sqrt{9} = 3$

9. $\sqrt{169} = 13$
10. $\sqrt{121} = 11$
11. $\sqrt{324} = 18$
12. $\sqrt{289} = 17$

13. $\sqrt{16} = 4$
14. $\sqrt{196} = 14$
15. $\sqrt{400} = 20$
16. $\sqrt{144} = 12$

17. $\sqrt{64} = 8$
18. $\sqrt{256} = 16$
19. $\sqrt{225} = 15$
20. $\sqrt{25} = 5$

Total Problems _20_ Problems Correct ___

# Answer Key

---

Name_____      Skill: Square Roots

Find the square roots.

1.  $\sqrt{784} = 28$    2. $\sqrt{196} = 14$    3. $\sqrt{144} = 12$    4. $\sqrt{900} = 30$

5.  $\sqrt{121} = 11$    6. $\sqrt{625} = 25$    7. $\sqrt{225} = 15$    8. $\sqrt{64} = 8$

9.  $\sqrt{100} = 10$    10. $\sqrt{256} = 16$    11. $\sqrt{441} = 21$    12. $\sqrt{400} = 20$

13. $\sqrt{484} = 22$    14. $\sqrt{49} = 7$    15. $\sqrt{529} = 23$    16. $\sqrt{36} = 6$

17. $\sqrt{81} = 9$    18. $\sqrt{25} = 5$    19. $\sqrt{289} = 17$    20. $\sqrt{16} = 4$

Total Problems __20__ Problems Correct ____

89

---

Name_____      Skill: Exponents

Find the powers.

1.  $3^3 = 27$    2. $7^2 = 49$    3. $4^3 = 64$    4. $6^3 = 216$

5.  $2^3 = 8$    6. $5^3 = 125$    7. $8^3 = 512$    8. $9^3 = 729$

9.  $1^3 = 1$    10. $8^4 = 4,096$    11. $6^4 = 1,296$    12. $2^4 = 16$

13. $5^4 = 625$    14. $9^4 = 6,561$    15. $3^4 = 81$    16. $5^4 = 625$

Total Problems __16__ Problems Correct ____

90

---

Name_____      Skill: Exponents

Find the powers.

1.  $5^3 = 125$    2. $2^2 = 4$    3. $1^3 = 1$    4. $3^3 = 27$

5.  $4^3 = 64$    6. $8^3 = 512$    7. $6^3 = 216$    8. $7^3 = 343$

9.  $10^3 = 1,000$    10. $9^4 = 6,561$    11. $1^4 = 1$    12. $5^4 = 625$

13. $3^4 = 81$    14. $8^5 = 32,768$    15. $5^4 = 625$    16. $2^4 = 16$

Total Problems __16__ Problems Correct ____

91

---

Name_____      Skill: Exponents

Find the powers.

1.  $7^3 = 343$    2. $4^2 = 16$    3. $5^3 = 125$    4. $3^3 = 27$

5.  $1^3 = 1$    6. $9^3 = 729$    7. $8^3 = 512$    8. $7^4 = 2,401$

9.  $2^3 = 8$    10. $8^4 = 4,096$    11. $5^4 = 625$    12. $3^2 = 9$

13. $6^5 = 7,776$    14. $3^6 = 729$    15. $2^5 = 32$    16. $7^5 = 16,807$

Total Problems __16__ Problems Correct ____

92

     119

# Answer Key

---

Name_____          Skill: Exponents

Find the powers.

1. $2^6 = 64$      2. $8^7 = 2,097,152$   3. $4^6 = 4,096$     4. $9^6 = 531,441$

5. $3^7 = 2,187$   6. $4^7 = 16,384$   7. $8^6 = 262,144$   8. $5^6 = 15,625$

9. $7^7 = 823,543$   10. $2^7 = 128$   11. $3^6 = 729$   12. $5^4 = 625$

13. $6^7 = 279,936$   14. $1^5 = 1$   15. $2^5 = 32$   16. $7^4 = 2,401$

Total Problems _16_ Problems Correct ____

© Carson-Dellosa CD-3750          93

---

Name_____          Skill: Exponents

Find the powers.

1. $3^6 = 729$   2. $4^5 = 1,024$   3. $2^5 = 32$   4. $6^6 = 46,656$

5. $10^5 = 100,000$   6. $6^5 = 7,776$   7. $10^6 = 1,000,000$   8. $1^4 = 1$

9. $8^6 = 262,144$   10. $2^6 = 64$   11. $3^5 = 243$   12. $4^6 = 4,096$

13. $11^6 = 1,771,561$   14. $8^5 = 32,768$   15. $5^7 = 78,125$   16. $11^5 = 161,051$

Total Problems _16_ Problems Correct ____

© Carson-Dellosa CD-3750          94

---

Name_____          Skill: Exponents

Find the powers.

1. $2^7 = 128$   2. $4^7 = 16,384$   3. $3^6 = 729$   4. $7^7 = 823,543$

5. $5^7 = 78,125$   6. $6^6 = 46,656$   7. $9^6 = 531,441$   8. $6^7 = 279,936$

9. $5^6 = 15,625$   10. $4^6 = 4,096$   11. $2^6 = 64$   12. $9^7 = 4,782,969$

13. $12^7 = 35,831,808$   14. $7^6 = 117,649$   15. $3^7 = 2,187$   16. $4^5 = 1,024$

Total Problems _16_ Problems Correct ____

© Carson-Dellosa CD-3750          95

---

Name_____          Skill: Finding Exponents

Complete the chart.

| Base number | Second Power | Third Power | Fourth Power | Fifth Power | Sixth Power |
|---|---|---|---|---|---|
| 1 | 1 | 1 | 1 | 1 | 1 |
| 2 | 4 | 8 | 16 | 32 | 64 |
| 3 | 9 | 27 | 81 | 243 | 729 |
| 4 | 16 | 64 | 256 | 1,024 | 4,096 |
| 5 | 25 | 125 | 625 | 3,125 | 15,625 |
| 6 | 36 | 216 | 1,296 | 7,776 | 46,656 |
| 7 | 49 | 343 | 2,401 | 16,807 | 117,649 |
| 8 | 64 | 512 | 4,096 | 32,768 | 262,144 |
| 9 | 81 | 729 | 6,561 | 59,049 | 531,441 |
| 10 | 100 | 1,000 | 10,000 | 100,000 | 1,000,000 |

Total Problems _10_ Problems Correct ____

© Carson-Dellosa CD-3750          96

© Carson-Dellosa CD-3750          120

Multiply.

$$423 \times 6$$

Divide.

$$4\overline{)681}$$

Change to simplest form.

$$\frac{48}{52} =$$

Multiply.

$$\frac{2}{5} \times \frac{2}{5} =$$

Multiply.

$$103 \times 294$$

Divide.

$$63\overline{)4,473}$$

Change to simplest form.

$$\frac{48}{36} =$$

Multiply.

$$3 \times 5\frac{1}{5} =$$

Multiply.

$$7,510 \times 50$$

Divide.

$$75\overline{)2,700}$$

Change to an improper fraction.

$$6\frac{1}{5}$$

Multiply.

$$4\frac{1}{5} \times 5\frac{1}{2} =$$

Divide.

$$9\overline{)45}$$

Change to simplest form.

$$\frac{49}{56} =$$

Multiply.

$$\frac{1}{5} \times \frac{5}{6} =$$

Divide.

$$\frac{3}{4} \div \frac{13}{16} =$$

5

$375,500$

$30,282$

$2,538$

$\dfrac{7}{8}$

36

71

170 r1

$\dfrac{1}{6}$

$\dfrac{31}{5}$

$1\dfrac{1}{3}$

$\dfrac{12}{13}$

$\dfrac{12}{13}$

$23\dfrac{1}{10}$

$15\dfrac{3}{5}$

$\dfrac{4}{25}$

Find the greatest common factor.

$72, 90$ _____

© CD-3750

---

Subtract.

$$\frac{3}{5} - \frac{1}{5} =$$

© CD-3750

---

Add.

$$\begin{array}{r} 3.35 \\ .01 \\ + \ 4.60 \\ \hline \end{array}$$

© CD-3750

---

Subtract.

$$\begin{array}{r} 4.31 \\ - \ \ .4 \\ \hline \end{array}$$

© CD-3750

---

Divide.

$$5\frac{1}{4} \div 1\frac{1}{8} =$$

© CD-3750

---

Add.

$$\frac{1}{6} + \frac{5}{8} =$$

© CD-3750

---

Add.

$$\begin{array}{r} 21.5 \\ + \ 2.9 \\ \hline \end{array}$$

© CD-3750

---

Subtract.

$$\begin{array}{r} .45 \\ - \ .21 \\ \hline \end{array}$$

© CD-3750

---

Divide.

$$5 \div 3\frac{2}{5} =$$

© CD-3750

---

Add.

$$\frac{1}{4} + \frac{3}{5} =$$

© CD-3750

---

Subtract.

$$\begin{array}{r} 5 \ \ \\ - \ \frac{3}{5} \\ \hline \end{array}$$

© CD-3750

---

Add.

$$18.4 + .06 =$$

© CD-3750

---

Divide.

$$\frac{1}{2} \div \frac{4}{9} =$$

© CD-3750

---

Find the greatest common factor.

$48, 56$ _____

© CD-3750

---

Subtract.

$$\begin{array}{r} 3 \ \ \\ - \ \frac{3}{4} \\ \hline \end{array}$$

© CD-3750

---

Add.

$$5.15 + 17.623 =$$

© CD-3750

18

$\frac{2}{5}$

7.96

3.91

$4\frac{2}{3}$

$\frac{19}{24}$

24.4

.24

$1\frac{8}{17}$

$\frac{17}{20}$

$4\frac{2}{5}$

18.46

$1\frac{1}{8}$

8

$2\frac{1}{4}$

22.773

Multiply.

$$88.4 \times 13.5$$

Change to a percentage.

$$\frac{1}{4} =$$

Solve.

$$8\% \text{ of } 80 =$$

Solve.

88 is 110% of _____

Multiply.

$$.611 \times 110$$

Change to a decimal.

$$30\% =$$

Solve.

$$17\% \text{ of } 20 =$$

Solve.

4 is 25% of _____

Multiply.

$$.2 \times 5$$

Divide.

$$.3\overline{)3.15}$$

Change to a percentage.

.59

Solve.

120 is _____% of 160

Multiply.

$$.06 \times 5$$

Divide.

$$8\overline{).88}$$

Change to a percentage.

87.5

Solve.

10 is _____% of 100

| | | | |
|---|---|---|---|
| 1,193.4 | 25% | 6.4 | 80 |
| 67.21 | .3 | 3.4 | 16 |
| 1 | 10.5 | 59% | 75 |
| .30 | .11 | 8,750% | 10 |

Solve.

$3 \times (16 + {}^-27) =$

© CD-3750

Add.

$27 + {}^-18 =$

© CD-3750

Subtract.

$30 - {}^-20 =$

© CD-3750

Multiply.

$6 \times {}^-5 =$

© CD-3750

---

Solve.

$(6 + 5) \times 2 + 3 =$

© CD-3750

Add.

$15 + {}^-72 =$

© CD-3750

Subtract.

$50 - 30 =$

© CD-3750

Multiply.

$9 \times {}^-3 =$

© CD-3750

---

Solve.

$(25 \times 6) + 17 =$

© CD-3750

Add.

$90 + {}^-71 =$

© CD-3750

Subtract.

$10 - 2 =$

© CD-3750

Solve.

$36 + 14 - {}^-31 =$

© CD-3750

---

Solve.

$36 \div (3 \times 3) =$

© CD-3750

Add.

$2 + {}^-7 =$

© CD-3750

Subtract.

$4 - {}^-1 =$

© CD-3750

Solve.

$1 + 15 - {}^-4 =$

© CD-3750

-30  50  9  129

-27  20  -57  25

81  8  19  167

20  5  -5  4

**Multiply.**

$21 \times {}^-16 =$

© CD-3750

---

**Solve.**

If $t = 3$, then

$12 + t =$

© CD-3750

---

**Solve.**

If $y = 9$, then

$8 + y =$

© CD-3750

---

**Solve using the following values: $g = 8$ and $i = 24$**

$i \div g =$

© CD-3750

---

**Find the value of the variable.**

$w + 36 = 39$

© CD-3750

---

**Multiply.**

$14 \times {}^-2 =$

© CD-3750

---

**Solve.**

If $e = 31$, then

$88 - e =$

© CD-3750

---

**Solve using the following values: $f = 6$ and $j = 12$**

$j \div f =$

© CD-3750

---

**Find the value of the variable.**

$27 = 9 \times k$

© CD-3750

---

**Multiply.**

$21 \times {}^-4 =$

© CD-3750

---

**Solve.**

If $c = 12$, then

$36 \div c =$

© CD-3750

---

**Solve where $z = 5$.**

$4z =$

© CD-3750

---

**Find the value of the variable.**

$14 = 8 + x$

© CD-3750

---

**Solve.**

If $x = 7$, then

$7 - x =$

© CD-3750

---

**Solve using the following values: $b = 3$ and $d = 5$.**

$b \times d =$

© CD-3750

---

**Find the value of the variable.**

$12 = 5 + r$

© CD-3750

3

3

17

15

3

2

57

-336

6

20

3

-28

7

15

0

-84

Solve.

$$4 + x = 8$$

Find the square root.

$$\sqrt{81} =$$

Solve.

$$3^7 =$$

Solve.

$$9^6 =$$

Solve.

$$30 = 7 + x$$

Solve.

$$15^2 =$$

Solve.

$$7^3 =$$

Solve.

$$6^6 =$$

Solve.

$$a + 16 = 37$$

Solve.

$$5^2 =$$

Find the square root.

$$\sqrt{121} =$$

Solve.

$$5^7 =$$

Solve.

$$5 + x = 8$$

Solve.

$$2^2 =$$

Find the square root.

$$\sqrt{1} =$$

Solve.

$$10^5 =$$

| 4 | 9 | 2,187 | 531,441 |
|---|---|---|---|
| 23 | 225 | 343 | 46,656 |
| 21 | 25 | 11 | 78,125 |
| 3 | 4 | 1 | 100,000 |